WINDOWS

WINDOWS

THE COMPLETE ART
OF WINDOW TREATMENT

JOCASTA INNES

PRACTICAL INSTRUCTIONS BY
CASSANDRA KENT

Orbis · London

First published in Great Britain by
Orbis Publishing Corporation
A division of Macdonald & Co (Publishers) Ltd
A BPPC plc Company

Produced and designed by Shuckburgh Reynolds Ltd.
289 Westbourne Grove, London W11 2QA

British Library Cataloguing in Publication Data

Innes, Jocasta
    Windows.
    1. Windows   2. Interior decoration
    I. Title
    747′.3   NK 2121

ISBN 1-85155-070-4

Designed by Nigel Partridge
Picture research by Jenny de Gex & Tony Sattin
Artwork by Andrew Farmer

Typeset by SX Composing, Rayleigh, Essex
Reproduction by Fotographics Ltd
Printed and bound in Italy

Captions to photographs

PAGE 2: This detail from an old French window shows
how attractive decorated glass can look treated in a
purely secular style. The formal grid of lead cames binds
together a lively patchwork of decorated panes,
different in both treatment and subject matter.

RIGHT: Neo-Classical meets American vernacular in this
trio of pedimented windows in the clapboard wall of a
South Carolina house. The carved hoods are imposingly
Classical but it is the subtle play on horizontals – wide
boards alternating with fine shutter louvres – which give
such an austerely elegant effect.

PAGE 6: This unusual awning/shutter in the dining room
of a Turkish villa, or yalé, serves a dual purpose: to keep
out direct sunlight while reflecting the cool, wavering
light off the Bosporus on to the room's ceiling.

CONTENTS

8

There are many ways of looking at windows. Children draw houses like faces, with windows for eyes. Architects talk about the rhythms of fenestration, the balance between voids and solids. Housewives worry about the cost of curtaining, and the problem of keeping all that glass sparkling. Small boys get wicked joy throwing stones. Heating engineers are preoccupied by energy losses when windows are thrown open, while the medical profession speculates on possible health hazards when windows are kept sealed. Some housebuyers will spend thousands putting the windows back to their original state, while others will spend almost as much replacing original windows with sheets of plate glass.

Ladies leaning out of high windows are an inspiration for poets, and everything about windows is material for painters: the view from the window, the light falling inside, the silhouettes of people standing in front of them, the idea of windows as frames within a frame. Some decorators dress windows up, with lace petticoats and flounced curtains as elaborate as ball gowns, while others strip them to essentials with surrounds of stainless steel and blinds of natural canvas. Men look out of windows at pretty girls and pretty girls are always looking into windows at themselves. The right window can sell a house: picture windows in suburbia, windows with fretted balconies in seaside towns, little old crooked windows in country villages.

Windows are about light, views and status. What we tend to forget is that they are also about making connections. Through their windows buildings connect with visitors, passers by, the life of the street or square, the time of day and the passing of the seasons. Windows are the interface between the little world inside a house and the large world outside. The unguardedness of windows, so many apertures in our house walls, is based on all sorts of assumptions about the society we live in. We assume that people will abide by certain unwritten rules; that they will not stand outside staring in, or throw stones, or mistake an open window for an invitation to climb in. In a civilised society windows symbolise mutual trust and respect. As communities feel more secure, they proliferate windows. The huge windows of early Victorian villas, fronting the street, tell us a lot about the confidence of that period, while the small windows slotted into street elevations in so many housing schemes today tell us something about the problems of the society we live in now.

EYES ON THE WORLD

"Windows now threw rooms open to gardens, parks and distant views, and in towns to the flowing colour and life of streets. The rediscovery that windows had a two-way function, to admit light to a room and to give visual pleasure, indicated that Europeans were acquiring a healthier and more reasonable idea of the art of living."

The Architectural Interpretation of History
John Gloag

——TECHNOLOGY——

In the beginning, of course, there were almost certainly no windows at all. The first human habitations of any permanence had a door and a hole in the roof to let the smoke out. Safety and shelter were the priorities. Opening up holes in the walls not only breached one's defenses but let in the elements and other undesirables ranging from insects and rodents to hostile humans. Most of the earliest purpose built dwellings which have been excavated, in China and the Middle East, are closer to burrows and caves, partly dug into the ground, and then roofed over with mud-plastered bundles of reeds bent to form a shallow dome. These date from prehistoric times. Primitive people still build this way, especially where the climate is extreme, fiercely hot or cold.

The dawn of civilization brought many benefits,

9

LEFT: *One of the most original features of architectural writer Charles Jencks' astonishing theme house is this cushioned seating space at one end of the Summer Room. Sun rays carved into the floor and summery colours inspired by Poussin's painting* Dance to the Music of Time *reinforce the summer theme, while sliding windows open the space up on warm days to make a solar directly connected to the sunny garden.*

among them windows. Not that the first windows would have been much more than functional spy holes, rough openings set high up and sealed against intruders or the weather with a stone slab or a flap of hide. Noah's ark had just one window, as the Bible relates. "And it came to pass after forty days, that Noah opened the window of the ark." When social conditions are right, though, people feel secure enough and have enough leisure to attend to other things than survival. By classical times the desirability of windows was well understood. The gaily painted terraced houses in the Cretan capital of Knossos were pierced with row upon row of windows, unglazed but made into a noticeable feature with broad painted 'frames', just as many Mediterranean houses still are today. Life felt good to the Cretans, and their joie de vivre is evident in their sensuous wall painting, their love of warm, glowing colour, the open construction of buildings such as the palace, a place of open galleries and loggias open wide to sun and air and views over the sea.

Window technology advanced steadily, particularly under the practical Romans, but though they knew about glazing as well as windows – bronze circular window frames set with thick greenish glass were excavated at Pompeii – these tended to be restricted to patrician homes like the magnificent villa Pliny the Younger designed for himself with views in three different directions over the sea. Apartment buildings were quite common in Roman cities, but most citizens lived in houses built around a central open courtyard, where natural light flooding in made further windows unnecessary. Solid bourgeois houses like the surgeon's house at Pompeii turned their backs on the street, much as houses in an Arab medina tend to do today.

The Romans took their window technology with them to the northern outposts of the Empire, and the Roman villa at St Albans had glazed windows set into frescoed walls. After the Roman Empire fell apart it was many centuries before glazed windows were seen again, and then only in ecclesiastical buildings. Buildings did have windows, but these were small, set deep into thick walls and generally protected by an iron grid, or a trellis of canes or laths embedded in the plaster. These kept out birds, cats and marauders. Detachable wooden or stone shutters pivoting on metal pegs kept out wind and rain and – in some instances – invaders. Sometimes these were pierced to let in a little light. Even when glazing was first introduced into English domestic buildings around the fourteenth century, often only the upper segment was glazed, while the bottom was closed off with shutters. Primitive window arrangements like these could be seen in peasant cottages until well into the nineteenth century, though in some cases makeshift glazing was supplied by pieces of horn, mica or oiled cloth.

By Tudor times glazing was quite standard in aristocratic and wealthy bourgeois houses. The typical Tudor window was a casement, of outward opening type, made up of many small panes of blown glass held together by lead cames. A 'came' is a lead strip, deeply grooved either side, into which glass pieces can be slotted. Soft enough to bend easily and weather resistant, lead cames are still used in making stained glass windows. Lead is not rigid, however, and lattice paned Tudor windows had either to be quite small or reinforced by being set in sturdy frames of wood, as in the Long Gallery at Little Moreton Hall, dated around 1570, or in stone mullions and transoms.

Tudor builders devised new window types, such as the oriel (from the Latin *oratoriolum*, or little prayer place) projecting like a decorative swallow's nest, and precursor of the later bow window, and the dormer window, highly practical

ABOVE: The more primitive a building, especially in harsh climates, the smaller and fewer the windows. Two little 'wind eyes' set into thick stone walls give just enough light and ventilation to this small croft on an exposed Hebridean headland.

ABOVE: *The romance of the age of chivalry lives on in Catherine de Valois' recently restored 'Chambre de Retrait' in Leeds Castle, Kent. Double ogive windows enhanced by a decorative quatrefoil are set into a deep embrasure scooped in the thickness of 12th century stonework.*

OVERLEAF: *The monumental scale of Hardwick Hall in Derbyshire makes this Elizabethan prodigy house a truly fitting symbol of a daring and virile age. Built by Robert Smythson for the redoubtable Bess of Hardwick, the house rapidly became legendary for its extravagant use of glazing.*

because it allowed light to be introduced into the sloping roofs of the loft, or 'dormitorium', in so many old wooden houses and cottages. They could also cope with windows on a grand scale, like the ones Bess of Hardwick ordered for Hardwick Hall, mullioned windows of such prodigious height that awed contemporaries made up ballads and ditties celebrating 'Hardwick Hall – more glass than wall'. Tudor smiths and carpenters were skilled craftsmen, and their stepped gables, framed in carved oak, and beautifully wrought iron latches and frames, were as handsome as the glazed and bellying poops of a man o' war. But though refinements crept in, window technology as such did not make a leap forward till the early seventeenth century, with the introduction of sliding wooden vertical sashes. The word sash is a corruption of 'chassis', denoting a wood frame rather than a leaded light.

——Sash Windows——

Sash windows had many advantages. They obtained their rigidity from wooden frames, set with glazed panes, both cheaper than stone mullions and stronger than leaded lights. Sashes meant that windows could grow in size without being exorbitantly costly. Conveniently, sashes could be exactly proportioned to replace old casements. Really narrow casements were fitted with an ingenious variation on the sash, horizontally sliding in grooves like some old shutters. But the real appeal of the sash window was aesthetic. Not only did they open up vistas and flood interiors with light (thus causing many stately homes to be constructed facing north, to check the fading action of the sun on furnishings

and carpets), but their elegant, regular grid of glazing bars was ideally suited to the neo-classical style of building which replaced the English vernacular at around this time as the proper style for the homes of gentlemen, or aspiring gentlemen. No one knows for certain where sash construction orginated; France and Holland have both been credited with their invention though they were known as 'Italian windows'. Early sash windows were set flush with the wall and had substantial glazing bars, an inch thick or more. The upper sashes were fixed, only the lower part moving up and down. Interestingly, Sir Christopher Wren varied his sashes at Hampton Court with slightly bevelled panes tinted faintly in pink and lilac. Rose coloured spectacles on a massive scale.

So popular were sashes that government found it profitable to levy a window tax, the first being instituted in 1695, to the annoyance of good citizens. "For it is a dreadful thing to pay as we do," one innkeeping lady of the time protested. "Why now there is above forty shillings for window lights, and yet we have stopped up all we could; we have almost blinded the house, I am sure." The tax was profitable enough to be repeated seven times and to this day bricked up eighteenth century windows remain as a legacy in many old streets, wall-eyed and disconcerting.

As sash window construction grew more refined, glazing bars grew more delicate, the panes grew larger and the internal joinery became more elegant and artful. The sash window reached its acme in the early days of Victoria's reign. Immense sash windows took up most of the wall of the reception rooms in the new semi-detached

14

ABOVE: *Crown glass panes have an almost facetted glitter set into an oriel type window, of timber construction, projecting from an old, mellow wall of black stained beams and herringbone brickwork. Windows like these evolved into the gracefully curved Georgian bow window.*

RIGHT: *Tall narrow windows in old houses often lend themselves to the addition of a window seat beneath, set into the thickness of the wall. Panelled shutters, and slender curtains hitched up into swags either side, are adequate window dressing in this elegant early 19th century house in Charleston, Carolina.*

villas and suburban terraced houses. Sometimes they were hung with coquettish balconies of wooden lattice, or wrought iron. Internally, the painted pine surrounds were beautifully put together, their shutter boxes splayed to reflect more light outwards. The wooden shutters were closed at night, for warmth and sound insulation, and also of course for security – great windows opening so near to the streets must have been tantalising to the small-time criminals described by contemporary writers like Charles Dickens and Christopher Mayhew.

Had it not been for two important innovations towards the end of the nineteenth century, it is not impossible that window design would have remained happily eclectic, in the Victorian manner, with Italianate, mock Gothic, mock Queen Anne and a salad of other styles alternating along city streets according to the taste of architect and client. After all, window design had not essentially altered in the previous two thousand years. Whatever their shape, size or construction, windows remained subordinate to walls, eyes stuck in a face. But the invention of cheap 'float' glass production, together with cantilever construction and the patent glazing developed by the Duke of Devonshire's extraordinary head gardener, Joseph Paxton, for the Crystal Palace, coalesced to give window technology such an almighty shove that the whole history of architecture altered course in consequence.

─────── MASS PRODUCTION ───────

Mass production of glass meant that glass could be obtained quite cheaply in large sheets, unlike the old mouth blown 'crown' glass panes which had been used for domestic glazing, and whose maximum size was 24×15 ins (60×37.5 cm). One result of the new float or plate glass coming on the market was that there was a rush to replace the old many-paned sashes with single paned ones, the Victorian precursor of the picture window. These were certainly easier to clean, and allowed an uninterrupted view, but aesthetically their invasion of the precise geometry of eighteenth century façades was a disaster. Too late, people recognised that the finely chequered spaces created by the old many pane sashes in a plain brick façade were the one element which brought them to life.

As with all questions of proportion, an apparently trifling change in scale can make all the difference. For an example of this one has only to compare a twinkling, benign Queen Anne housefront with the utilitarian grimness of a nineteenth century mill or warehouse. Both make use of rows of identical windows in a plain brick façade, but with utterly different effect. Plate glass may have opened up the view from inside, but from outside the neat eighteenth century façades were ruined.

In retrospect this seems like the bad news. The good news about mass produced glass is that it encouraged glazing on a much more adventurous scale. There was an immediate mushrooming of glassed-in conservatories and garden rooms on houses of any pretension, paralleled by handsome new glazed shopping arcades in important shopping centres. In effect houses made up of windows, these pointed the way innovative architects were soon to go.

The pioneer of glazing on a monumental scale was undoubtedly Paxton. Not only was the Crystal Palace, built to house the Great Exhibition of 1851, spectacularly large and awesomely novel, an audacious bubble of a building, but the speed of its construction – a mere seventeen weeks – marked it out to any thoughtful observer as a portent of a new age. Paxton succeeded because he had rationalised construction methods to take advantage of mass production. The whole palace was put together from standardised spans of cast-iron ribbing, designed to take pre-cut sheets of glass. What makes this ancestor of pre-cast concrete and other modern mass-produced building methods so striking is that it was designed, in an age of pre-eminent engineers, by a man with no engineering or architectural qualifications. Paxton had learnt his lessons designing glasshouses for Chatsworth.

─────── WALLS OF DAYLIGHT ───────

The man who took the step that exploded all our preconceptions about windows in relation to buildings was a young German architect, Walter Gropius. In 1911 he designed a factory at Alfeld in which a glass and metal skin, non-constructional unlike Paxton's iron cage, was cantilevered out from the floors and wrapped around an entire building, like a continuous window. No longer windows in walls, but windows *as* walls – 'walls of   17

LEFT: *One transparent wall, in this case facing into a garden, gives this small family house, by architect Birkin Heyward, something of the fascination of an old fashioned doll's house, as well as making the most of available light and space.*

daylight' as they were lyrically described. It was the first really big jump in architectural thinking for centuries, and this time the message was received loud and clear by all the leading architects of the day from Le Corbusier to Alvar Aalto. Gropius' aim had been to subtilise the transition between indoors and outdoors, and give the workplace a new dignity by setting it in a privileged context, light and open instead of dark and shut away as the old nineteenth century industrial buildings had been.

Curtain walling, as this method of construction came to be known, after the enclosing walls of medieval castles, quite rapidly established itself as the distinctive and desirably modern method of construction, especially for commercial and public buildings on a large scale. The majority of the most celebrated twentieth century buildings, such as the Seagram building, have been glass and steel towers, of ever increasing tapering height and streamlined elegance. It is surely no accident that nearly all of them are in New York, because almost from the start Modernism was welcomed enthusiastically by the new world. Glass towers not only satisfied an urge to think big, they had practical advantages over the old style skyscrapers, being quicker and cheaper to build. Glass towers also have problems, which we shall discuss presently,

18

ABOVE: *Like a fanlight taken to the power of ten, this immense arched window provides a suitably heroic visual frame to a sweep of blue ocean in the Lawson House, Quoque, New York, designed by Robert Stern. Simple furnishings, an absence of clutter, ensure that the room stays focussed on the view.*

but they are still, more than seventy years after Gropius' Fagus factory, the favourite of all commercial building types. Today's versions tend to be sleeker than ever, almost seamless boxes of glass now often tinted blue, or bronze, or darkened like sunglasses, or mirrored one way, so people can see out but no one can look in.

Domestic architecture was less dramatically affected by the new glass-and-steel 'walls of daylight' philosophy, perhaps because many people feel vulnerable and exposed living in glass boxes, although they may enjoy working in them. All the same, affected it undoubtedly was, in all sorts of ways. All glass might be going too far, but partly glass was almost mandatory in houses designed during the twenties and thirties, at the height of the craze for glass walls, bricks and roofs. The Maison de Verre in Paris, a box of glass bricks which looks like a cube of light at night, is one of the most celebrated domestic examples, and still standing unspoilt thanks to a campaign mounted in the last couple of years to save it for the nation. Odd, even a little inelegant seen from outside by day, the Maison de Verre rejoices in a serenely diffused and steady light inside; with its great reaches of translucent wall it is a peaceful place.

Mies van der Rohe and Frank Lloyd Wright were two internationally famous architects who incorporated the new glass technology into their domestic scale buildings. Mies van der Rohe's Farnsworth House, a streamlined transparent package of immense sophistication come to rest, incongruously, in rough pastureland, uses glass as the Japanese might use oiled paper screens. Surprising, ethereal to look at, it is reputedly hot as a furnace inside in summer. Frank Lloyd Wright's buildings are more eclectic, using traditionally scaled windows in some places, and whole walls of sliding glass doors in others. The Hanna house, for instance, has sliding doors that melt away in fine weather so that one whole section of the house merges with the sunny terrace outside. In winter, however, the doors are closed and central heating plus sun entering via the glass doors keeps the place perfectly warm.

Another glass innovation which many architects, notably Le Corbusier, introduced into their houses, was the corner window. Glazing round a corner is a dramatic device because it challenges one of our oldest assumptions about the structures we inhabit, which is that corners are in a sense columns, which carry the weight of the roof. Dissolving the corner with a continuous window, cantilevered out, has a powerful spatial effect because the diagonal is the most powerful release from a room. Metal framed corner windows, often curved, remain as a legacy of Le Corbusier's style in many seaside suburbs, often associated with white, rough cast plaster walls and turquoise tiling – hacienda style. The maestro of the corner window, crafted like a Fabergé box, was the Italian architect Carlo Scarpa, and it is probably due to the influence of his work that we have the latest idea in glass corners, where two mitred sheets of glass are sealed with resin to make the closest thing to an invisible corner, a touch of showmanship which seems especially suited to boutique windows.

At what one might call high street level, the ubiquitous legacy of the inter-war infatuation with glass is the picture window. Propagandists of glass, such as the artist Paul Nash, who designed a celebrated all-glass bathroom for the dancer Tilly Losch, admired it for its hygienic qualities and its slick shining surfaces where no germs could linger and uninterrupted streams of healthy sunlight could come pouring through. Coco Chanel, coincidentally, had popularised sunbathing and made suntanned skin newly chic. The rest and sunshine treatment for tuberculosis had further established light, air and sunshine as actively beneficial, flushing away disease like some cosmic disinfectant. Small wonder that outsize windows opening onto green prospects, however small, became a status symbol and mark of up-to-dateness. Unlike the carefully composed scenery framed by classical windows, today's picture window nearly always offers a random snap of nature, a Sickert painting as opposed to a Claude Lorrain. Picture not as in picturesque but as in snapshot.

CURRENT PROBLEMS AND NEW DIRECTIONS

Glassiness, on the scale of contemporary steel and glass towers, creates some problems for which architects are forever seeking solutions. Some of these are interesting because they indicate possible new directions in domestic design.

Glass buildings tend to become overheated in sunny weather, a problem which can be alleviated by air conditioning, but wastefully from the point of view of energy conservation. Sophisticated heat exchange systems, like the one used in Richard Rogers' controversial Lloyds building, draw heat generated between the layers of window glass directly into the building's exchange system, so that it can be used to heat water and perform other functions economically.

Ironically, considering their transparency, it is often difficult to light the inner core of many glass towers. One fashionable solution is to build them around an atrium, or inner courtyard, but even here there are problems because natural light only penetrates a few floors down, whereas the atrium in a modern tower may rise to fifty storeys. Norman Foster's Hongkong Bank building makes use of immense tilted mirrors on the roof, which catch the sunlight and reflect it down into the depths of the building. This notion of 'borrowing' natural light is already infiltrating into domestic design and, being reasonably cheap, seems likely to be used more and more to beam sunlight into underlit foyers or north facing rooms.

——— HEAT EXCHANGE ———

The evolution of windows in northern climates has inevitably been ruled by climatic considerations. Our enjoyment of light has always been tempered by respect for chancy weather and winter wind, wet and cold. Our windows have always tried to strike a balance between admitting more cheering sunshine and sealing out bitter wind and draughts; glazing, or double glazing, play a crucial role. In different climates, from dry Mediterranean to steamy tropical, windows have performed different functions and developed along different lines, with results as exotic as the pierced screens in North African Hammams, or as effortlessly ornamental as the trellis cages, unglazed but hung with rattan blinds, which enclose the front of so many West Indian or New Orleans style houses. Solutions arrived at to combat sultry climates and glaring midday sunshine do not often translate literally into temperate climates, but some of their notions are so attractive and different that they can prompt a new approach.

One idea, for instance, which could be more widely copied on sunny house fronts, is the glassed-in balcony, like an overgrown oriel window, which

one finds on many northern Spanish houses. Their climate is sunnier than ours, but sunny days are often bedevilled by keen winds. The glassed-in balcony, usually at first floor level, not only allows the family to adjust the windows so they get the sun's warmth without the wind, but acts as a sort of heat storage unit for the room behind, raising its temperature quite naturally by several degrees. In hot weather the situation is reversed as far as possible, with the balcony opened up but shaded by blinds and open windows at the far end of the rooms beyond creating a fresh through draught.

A similar instinctive wisdom about heat exchanging is exhibited by the characteristic Caribbean trelliswork cage, or verandah room, which makes such an attractive façade to older houses, from 'chattel houses' upwards. What the unglazed trellised balconies do is encourage the air to blow through freely, while preventing the sun's heat from reaching the house inside, all of which naturally helps to cool the interior. In the case of masonry inner walls, which naturally tend to retain some moisture, this works even better because the cool air working on the slight moisture content has a natural refrigerating effect. In cooler weather the rattan blinds which cover the openings in the trellising can be drawn up, and sunlight pours in to warm the balcony and the room inside.

A trellis balcony may seem to have moved a long way from the glazed aperture which we tend to think of as a window, but of course windows in hot countries frequently are unglazed, designed for ventilation in the first place and lighting secondarily. Glazing can be used in these conditions but only when the building is artificially cooled by air conditioning, which is expensive and in the light of recent medical thinking not altogether desirable. In private homes the traditional sort of cooling arrangement, using trellis or pierced screens or long louvred shutters to allow air to circulate freely while breaking the sun's glare, is currently held to be sounder practice. Wide verandahs which prevent the sun from reaching and heating up the house walls increase the effectiveness of this natural cooling system.

——— TRADITIONAL SOLUTIONS ———

The moral seems to be that it is sensible to look into traditional building styles before doing any

RIGHT: *Windows are for ventilation first and light second in hot climates. The arched windows ranging round this garden room in a Jamaican house are trellised but not glazed, to encourage the freest possible movement of air while filtering out some of the dazzling glare of a Caribbean noon.*

building or conversion work, because a great deal of hard won experience and common sense is often embedded in old ways and practices. Architects today are not so dismissive of local, vernacular building types as they used to be in the early euphoric phase of Modernism, when it seemed as if glass, steel and concrete must build a brave new world and people believed in progress. All sorts of events, from the energy crisis to concern over pollution and its effect on world ecology, have combined to shake their confidence in radiant cities. In addition, an uneasy awareness has crept in that the public at large seem to dislike radiant cities; tower blocks get a bad press, new towns are full of young people dying to get away, political architecture like Brasilia or Chandigarh has failed to move the world's imagination.

This crisis of confidence has meant, among other welcome signs of self-questioning, that the past has become respectable. The old ways of doing things and the reasons why they were adopted are being studied with new interest and respect. Some of the findings are predictable, for example the social truth that most families would choose a small house with a garden in preference to a flat high in the sky. Others are less so, like the undeniable vitality of many overcrowded urban areas, popular and successful despite noise, litter, lack of greenery and many other features which would once have got them written off as slums due for redevelopment.

The despised suburban semi, once seen as epitomising petit bourgeois rectitude, prissiness and lack of aesthetic flare, is now being extolled by writers like Alice Coleman as the ideal house type in an increasingly unpredictable, even threatening, social environment. The semi-detached house, in Alice Coleman's recent controversial study, emerges as the eighties version of the Englishman's castle, a compact building with a safe and secluded back garden where children can play, and a token patch of front garden overlooked by windows which allow householders to size up the looks and intentions of anyone who pushes open the gate and approaches the front door. The ideal window for the purpose, Miss Coleman suggests, is the one set obliquely to the path and gate, which allows one to make these observations unseen. This is the exact modern parallel, though Miss Coleman does not make the point, of the medieval

23

LEFT: *Lit up by night the small diamond shaped windows, scattered randomly over one curved wall, contribute to the house-as-sculpture effect of this Peruvian building, which is like a rather kitsch re-working of ideas Le Corbusier explored at Ronchamps. The one real window, please note, is a glass porthole.*

'squint' window set into the walls of castles and fortified manor houses, which allowed the inmates to observe new arrivals, galloping towards the drawbridge, when they were no more than a speck on the horizon.

———— ALL SHAPES AND SIZES ————

If all the windows situated above the average shopping street could be lined up for inspection at eye level, they would almost certainly turn out to be a multifarious bunch. Builders and architects, and their clients too, have been indulging in window shopping, or should it be swapping, for centuries. Certain styles of window seem to exercise a perennial fascination; they may go out of fashion for a few decades, since buildings are less ephemeral than fashions in clothes, but you can be certain that they will recur, modified to adapt them to contemporary building methods or materials, but still recognisable.

There are many reasons for this persistence of certain window types. Sometimes architects are indulging in classical allusions, to gratify their clients' wish to live in houses that look dignified, solid and impressive. Stuccoed villas with immense tiers of Italianate windows line the leafy residential streets of many cities. (Styles of window have been an Italian cultural export since classical times.) Sometimes a particular style of window becomes a bestseller because it performs a particular function better than any other. French windows, for instance, derive from the long glazed doors opening out of the grands salons of innumerable French hotels privés and chateaux. When the long windows are reflected in equally long mirrors on the walls opposite, as in the Galerie des Glaces at Versailles, the effect is truly spectacular. French windows combine the convenience of double doors with the luminosity of windows; their continued popularity, on every other patio extension, is easily understood. But there are also windows which seem to please only for their picturesqueness, or because their shape is profoundly, if mysteriously, satisfying.

The round window is the leading example of art for art's sake in fenestration. Classical buildings used circular windows, as we know from the bronze framed window excavated at Pompeii. Rose windows, many petalled rosettes of stone

24

RIGHT: *When the Sun King, Louis XIV, set out to dazzle, in the fabulous Galerie des Glaces at Versailles, he achieved a coup de theatre. A procession of tall French windows bounces light back from tall arched mirrors on the wall opposite as well as from a crystal forest of magnificent chandeliers.*

tracery set with stained glass, are the glory of many ancient cathedrals, Chartres in particular. Neo Classicism rediscovered the 'oeil de boeuf' window, now glazed and usually framed in handsome mouldings of stone or stucco, and it appears in great houses from Palladio onwards. Ultimately it descended the social scale as appealing architectural features always do, turning up in lighthearted versions made of wood, set into the mellow brickwork of small eighteenth century houses, or even cottages. The nineteenth century found the round window less attractive, possibly because a reaction against Neo Classicism had taken hold, but it reappears, tidily reduced to a metal framed porthole, in many houses influenced by the Modern movement. Just lately, round windows are enjoying a new vogue with the Post Modernists. Royalty studios, a sprightly new London office building in the Post Modern manner, which admirably dodges pomposity on the one hand and glum functionalism on the other, wears a row of large round windows on its street façade, like big glass buttons.

Round windows are popular in the first place because they are decorative, but also, perhaps, because roundness has always symbolised wholeness, perfection, the line without beginning or end. A Jungian would refer the cult of the round window to the archetypal mandala. A poet might imagine a link with ancient moon cults. The fact remains that round windows are not noticeably functional and are more difficult to install and to open; we have them because we enjoy them.

Pointed, or Gothic, windows seem to exercise a similar attraction. Clearly their shape derives from the pointed arch and people familiar with Perpendicular church architecture tend to refer them back to ecclesiastical models, but pointed arches are also a feature of Moorish architecture, so there may have been many influences at work in shaping this window type. Venice, a city of windows as well as canals, has a wonderful variety of pointed windows with a distinctly exotic, Moorish air to them. Versions of the pointed window recur in buildings of different countries at different periods, but perhaps nowhere more captivatingly than in the Gothic manner launched by light-hearted medievalists like Horace Walpole, author of *The Castle of Otranto*, who designed his own 'toy villa', Strawberry Hill, with Gothic windows in an attempt to suggest 'the gloomth of ancient abbeys'. Gloomth or not, Gothic windows caught on because they looked decorative and exotic, a playful relief from the austerely rectilinear sashes which epitomised the Georgian look. The prettiest Gothic windows feature intricate iron glazing bars, which look frivolous and decorative picked out in white, but which were undoubtedly intended as an allusion both to leaded lights and to mullions and transoms of carved stone.

Another window which inspired countless imitations was the medieval oriel. Originally, oriels were not so much windows as small, screened balconies projecting into the chapel of some great house, where the Lord and his family could hear mass without joining the common folk below. By Tudor times oriels, usually built of stone but sometimes also of timber, were popular as window seats where the ladies could embroider and sew in good natural light – windows all round – while looking out on the world going about its business below. Glass on three sides gives much more light

ABOVE: *Windows as well as water contribute to the glamour of Venice. Pearl of the Adriatic and gateway to the east, Venice's confluence of cultures is reflected in a dazzling variety of window styles. This slender window is topped by an exotic Saracen arch.*

RIGHT: *The northern Spanish climate can be cold and windy even while the sun shines. Glazed balconies, like these overgrown oriels on a house front in Segovia, are a clever solution, warmly sheltered as well as decorative, with their lively ironwork.*

ABOVE: *Classical allusions, playfully handled, are a distinguishing feature of Post Modernist buildings. The large window dominating this austere Long Island interior is the so-called Venetian window gone abstract. The clear panes are fixed, only the many paned sections open and close.*

than glass on one only, and the practicality of this arrangement in times when only the wealthy used wax candles and most people made do with tallow tapers was so telling that the romantic oriel rapidly developed into the more streamlined bow window, which has remained one of the most beloved of all window types right down to the present day. Bow windows·add charm to house fronts, are both quaint and practical, since they open up a sunny façade and simultaneously create a perfect location for a window seat. By comparison the bay window, its later relation, is a clumsier construction, roomier inside but inconvenient to use or curtain. A piano is probably the ideal piece of furniture to station in a bay window – and this was common practice in countless Victorian villas – but today there are more bay windows than pianos.

FUTURE TRENDS

It is interesting to speculate about which of today's contributions to the rich vocabulary of window types will emerge as tomorrow's classic, one of those charismatic combinations of shape, location and glass which capture the fancy of the public. Ironically, considering the sophistication of building and glass technology, most of the windows one sees going into new buildings are paraphrases of traditional models. But there are exceptions. Modern churches sometimes achieve extraordinary effects with glazing. There is Matisse's serene chapel in Vence, where windows are no more than panels of joyfully coloured glass, alternating with panels of masonry. There is a church in Finland, where the east wall is a clear sheet of glass opening out into a dark forest where the Crucifix stands, its human pathos brilliantly underlined by its position, in the open, among the trees. Carlo Scarpa's astonishingly positioned windows, dissolving unexpected portions of a room's anatomy, indicate one way windows may go, if there are the resources to fund such innovative elegance.

Another Italian window I remember admiring was as stark as a window could be, a towering sheet of plain glass set into the rough stone wall of a tower overlooking a magnificent view of the Tuscan hills. Its sheer size and lack of framing makes it twentieth century, as does its frank intention to devour a spectacular view sans bars, frame or irrelevancies. Charles Jenks' controversial London house has many intriguing window designs, but none so luxurious and astonishing as the glazed seating area – part oriel, part space capsule – where the glass slides away leaving one sitting in an indoor-outdoor space suspended like a cushioned nose cone just above a sunny green garden.

Fifty, thirty, even twenty years ago, it might have looked as if windows as such would soon be obsolete, swallowed up in walls of glass, ventilation problems solved by air conditioning. But this vision, which was always more of an architect's dream than a realistic proposition, has receded. The wheel has come full circle and windows are definitely reinstated as the architectural element above all others which a good designer must wrestle with. Good windows are, as they have always tended to be, a balance between decorativeness and usefulness, the feature that brings façades to life and gives them character, and at the same time brings light and air and sparkle to the rooms inside. Size is no longer the criterion; proportion, location, framing, subtler issues are uppermost. Nothing in excess was the philosopher's prescription for wise living. The room furnished with windows, a solid, secure box provided with transparent 'eyes' upon the world, seems like a wise mean between the windowless huts which the human race first built, and the glass boxes into which the Modernists hoped to guide us. People need to feel safe, enclosed, and at the same time free to communicate, neither cut nor shut off. Windows, all of them, from the Norman arrow slit to the wall of glass, do this for us. Windows are *civilised*.

Nothing reinforces the self importance of owning property so agreeably as making the sort of minor structural alterations lumped these days under the heading of 'home improvements'. There may be excellent practical reasons for altering the fabric of a building; but the underlying impetus surely comes from a natural, human desire to make one's mark, visibly, on the place where one lives. Windows, being at once conspicuous and structurally uncomplicated, have always been a prime target for home improvers. Adding new windows, enlarging or altering the shape or position of old ones, is a game that has been played for centuries. If one were able to compare plans or elevations of almost any vernacular building going back several hundred years, it is likely the fenestration would be the feature most frequently altered. Putting larger or more fashionable windows into a working building, like a farmhouse, was a sign of prosperity and an expression of social aspiration quite as much as a genuine improvement to the structure, admitting more light, opening out to attractive views, giving more dignity to the rooms inside. One would not quarrel with most of the old examples; the higgledy piggledy fenestration of so many old country buildings is often one of their great attractions, and anyone who owns a window type as charming as an 'oeil de boeuf', or Gothic, or an early and elegant bow window, must feel grateful to their predecessors.

It was in the late nineteenth century, with the advent of cheap float glass, that the trouble began. Replacing earlier types of glazing with large sheets of glass became a popular, cheap and easy way of updating a house. How nice to be able to look out unimpeded by glazing bars, and how much easier and quicker to keep these large panes bright and clean. A large number of old Georgian houses, whose finely judged window detailing is their chief architectural distinction, were vandalised as a result. To the inhabitants it may have seemed that simplifying their windows opened up new delights, but externally their buildings became as it were blinded, robbed of expression. When, as almost invariably happened, the inhabitants then found their privacy threatened and felt obliged to veil their improved up-to-date windows with net curtains, the effect was compounded. Georgian buildings may have suffered most from this insensitive modernising, but the craze for window swapping continues right down to the present day, often justified today as part of a double-glazing installation. A 'picture window' is still a selling feature in the estate agent's book, whether or not the picture the window frames is worth looking at. Stripped of their original busy, lively glazing patterns, the friendly façades of thirties semis lining the streets out of towns and villages acquire an air of steely inscrutability, like people wearing wraparound sunspecs. One in three terraced artisan cottages has its demure street front blown open by a mass-produced preformed 'bow window' complete with a couple of phony 'bull's eyes'. However, with the increasing attention being paid to conservation and a consequent re-evaluation of domestic architecture, however modest or recent, there seems to be a stirring of respect for old solutions and practices. More people are pausing to think out the pros and cons before calling in the double glazing contractor.

This is not to say that any alterations to existing

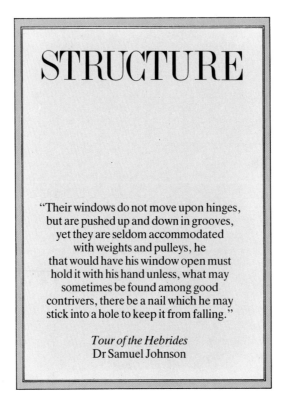

STRUCTURE

"Their windows do not move upon hinges, but are pushed up and down in grooves, yet they are seldom accommodated with weights and pulleys, he that would have his window open must hold it with his hand unless, what may sometimes be found among good contrivers, there be a nail which he may stick into a hole to keep it from falling."

Tour of the Hebrides
Dr Samuel Johnson

RIGHT: *One of the most self-indulgent ways to enjoy a view must be lying back in the bath, and in this sumptuously simple bathroom in the Dominican Republic, fashioned in the smoothly rounded adobe style, everything is directed towards the slice of glimmering blue beyond the tub.*

ABOVE: *Semicircular rooflights above tall sash windows, in this converted warehouse in Cambridge, give scale and symmetry to an otherwise undistinguished elevation, as well as flooding the interior with light. Note how expressive and face-like the wall is now with its arched eyebrows.*

windows are vandalistic. The very common improvement of opening up a back extension by installing glazed doors onto a paved area creates a civilised new relationship of indoor and outdoor which makes what used to be the dead end of many small terraced homes come alive, and gives city gardens a new dimension. Not all old spec building was so conscientiously designed that it cannot be improved upon; enlarging windows or adding new ones to favour a poky room, or make more of a sunny aspect, is good practice. Conversions of some old building types, such as barns, old schoolhouses, chapels and warehouses, invariably involves rethinking the existing fenestration. Putting rooflights and skylights into loft conversions, new extensions or old outbuildings can create dramatic and interesting new living spaces. Glass is a material which twentieth century technology handles with sophistication and daring, and we should not be afraid of using it. But a point to bear in mind when you are thinking about making window alterations is whether the end justifies the means. Most people would agree that house owners should be allowed to do what they like with the private face of their houses, within reason and with the approval of the building inspector. However, the street frontage, especially in terraced housing close to or opening directly onto the street, is different; the whole is greater than its parts in such schemes, and one insensitive, misjudged, so-called 'improvement' can spoil the unity of the whole street.

On the whole it is the cheaper houses in up-and-coming areas which suffer from reckless improvement, their potentially characterful bay windows and stucco ornamentation being ruthlessly suppressed in favour of metal framed plate glass by the first wave of new incumbents. It may be understandable too, because neglected streetscapes look grimy and forlorn enough to be a challenge to new brooms to make a clean sweep. The pity is, though, that it is not until three or four owners have done a more sympathetic job of restoration that the potential charm and visual sweep of the place becomes apparent. It is not just an aesthetic mistake to tamper with a street elevation, it can also be a financial one; as gentrification gets under way it is the genuine period article, its integrity unimpaired, which fetches the best price. This has happened often enough in London during the past twenty years, and continues to be the case, to make it a point worth emphasizing.

───── **PROFESSIONAL ADVICE** ─────

Getting an architect to advise on window changes or alterations is expensive but relieves the layperson of all sorts of worries, from obtaining planning permission to having some comeback if things go wrong, and you should end up with a sounder, more durable installation. This is an area where commonsense applies. If the change is small scale and simple, such as knocking a small extra window into a back room or extending an existing window to floor level, and you know of a good, reliable local building firm, you can usually go ahead safely without professional advice, especially if you are using standard windows or doors which should complement those already in place.

If you are thinking of making alterations which could weaken the structure, like enlarging an existing window by quite a bit, or knocking a large window through a windowless wall, you should consult an architect or quantity surveyor, who may ask for an engineer's calculations. Whether it is safe or not will depend on all sorts of considerations like the thickness of the walls, the height of the building and the size of the projected window. If you want to remove a large part of a structural wall you would almost certainly have to put in reinforcement in the way of concrete lintels or an RSJ. The same would apply if you wanted to put windows into a loft which involved cutting through any of the roof beams. A good builder could cope with installing the simpler sorts of roof light where nothing structural is being altered, but once you begin tampering with anything supportive, like rafters, you need qualified advice. This costs more, and certainly takes a lot longer, since their plans will need to be approved by the local planning office, but the warning tales one hears of walls cracking and bulging and roofs sagging and leaking where cowboy builders have been at work, suggest this is one game to play by the rules.

For large scale conversions, especially in a building with a strong character of its own, like a barn or a schoolhouse, you not only should get yourself an architect but make sure your architect has a good track record for sympathetic conversion work. Sympathetic need not mean unimaginative or

33

timid. In some cases a good architect might come up with something you would not have thought of, like a great shaft of a window in one end of a barn, but which still respects the integrity of the building. Working out a fenestration scheme which meets your requirements for light and ventilation, but which does not jibe with the existing character of the building, is a skilled job. The best results invariably arise from an intelligent collaboration between client and architect. You should expect to be able to talk through the plans, putting your needs clearly on record, and be satisfied that any decisions have your approval.

——— Choosing a Style ———

It has to be said that putting new windows into a building is powerfully exciting. Opening up solid walls, letting sunlight and air into a previously dark spot, maybe confronting a whole new view outside, is a thrilling exercise of droit de seigneur. It is one almost everyone living in an old house feels like indulging in, somewhere. "One of these days we are thinking of turning that window into French windows out onto the garden, and then we'll put a rooflight in the passage and make a much bigger room in the loft with a long window running along behind the parapet ..."

More than any previous century, the twentieth craves light. But light is too potent to be admitted thoughtlessly, on the principle that if some light is good more will always be better. The great blast of light from a picture window flattens all the life and character out of the sort of small cottage room where the light used to filter in through small, deep windows with wide sills. Rather than get all the extra light from one overscaled window it might be more subtle, and flattering to the room, to get it from one or two small new windows, pierced perhaps in unexpected places, so that sunlight can enter at different times.

Sheer size should never be the criterion, except where the view and/or the climate justifies thinking big and whole window walls are in order. Another aspect to be flexible about is shape. Windows need not be rectangular. In certain buildings, in particular sites, circular, half circular or pointed windows in the Gothic style would give great character as well as sufficient light. In others, one of the very modern constructions, like abstract

ABOVE: *Unexpectedness can be the making of a window, or a room.*
The kitchen in this converted mill in the Lot-et-Garonne has a lot going
for it in the way of picturesque beams, old tiles, and a green outlook,
but the stroke of genius was glazing in the archway and standing the
cooker in front. Together they make up a kitchen altar to the
household gods.

sculpture in glass, would be exciting as well as appropriate. Sometimes a window in a completely unexpected place, such as over a mantelpiece or kitchen stove, can make a room quite special. We have the technology to make a huge range of alternatives possible, and the most exciting solution may not be the most expensive.

Window alterations need to be thought through. One of the most exciting changes one can make to a ground floor room is to extend an existing window to ground floor level to make a glazed door or French window, giving onto a sunny, sheltered patch of garden or paved terrace. In summer this brings in the outdoors delightfully; overlooking one's garden from a window is a small pleasure compared with seeing it as a living continuation through open doors of the comforts and colours inside. But there are practical consequences to the creation of this new through-way. Security is an obvious one, an extra door to lock at night or when you leave the house. The family may start using this door as an easy way into the house, especially in summer, which not only means that muddy tracks will become a problem inside but a path may be beaten through any obstacles outside – it is a natural human tendency to take the shortest route between two points.

——— WINDOW SHOPPING ———

The range of standard windows available today covers most of the commonly used styles, from Georgian type sashes and metal framed, to sophisticated roof lights and dormers. These are cheaper to buy and usually to install as builders like working with familiar dimensions. If you want something to match existing windows which do not fall within standard ranges, you will have to get it made up by specialist joiners, which will cost more. Sash windows of the pre-Georgian type, with their smaller panes and thicker glazing bars, are a case in point. Possible sources of one-off windows are demolition yards and architectural salvage firms, which usually keep a large selection of old windows rescued in varying states of repair from demolished buildings. There is no guarantee that you will find an exact match to a period window, but these are good places to look for one-offs, window oddities, which can look wonderful when repaired and installed in the right place. I once bought an old Victorian Gothic style window, latticed panes in a pointed wooden frame, for a few pounds and had it fixed in the wall of a former cellar, which then became a basement room with a chapel-like atmosphere, and a poetic frame for a sweeping view of the Dorset coast. On the back wall of a not very distinguished turn of the century terrace house it looked unusual, but not out of place. A standard metal frame window, for instance, would have looked out of place and cost more.

One can get away with anachronisms in the window line when they are handsome in themselves. I would be tempted to buy any intrinsically attractive old window in a scrap yard – an oval, or round or Gothic – in the hopes of being able to fit it into a building somewhere, if I were in that happy stage of 'making improvements' to all but the most resolutely modern house. Interesting old windows seem to fit more happily into later houses than strikingly modern windows into old ones. But, of course, there are plenty of exceptions to this rule.   37

LEFT: *Where space permits, windows step out of their functional role and take on a sculptural importance in a room. Floating like a kite at the apex of a pointed window embrasure, the upper window makes good shapes with the conventional windows below.*

ABOVE: *Typical of the playful mood of late 18th century Gothic is this prettily pointed window, enlivened with tiny ruby panes, in 'The Convent', a picturesque house built by Henry Hoare the Second in 1765 on the carriage road to Stourhead.*

WINDOWS

Rugged old buildings can take uncompromisingly modern windows, when they are well designed. The London owner of an old brick brewhouse has turned a small roof into a terraced seating area reached via great glazed half circular doors, made from hardwood to fit the space. The chunkiness of the frame and the bold curve of the doors sit handsomely in the austerely workmanlike façade, and trap every ray of sunshine. I often wonder why old wooden cartwheels, pathetic bygones when propped up outside country pubs, are not glazed and set into country building conversions like a rustic version of a rose window. The skilled joinery that went into a wheelwright's creation is becoming a thing of the past, and their strength and delicacy would be fine to behold.

BASIC CONSIDERATIONS

I have already touched on the usual reasons for wanting to put in new windows, and some of the reasons for not rushing into such projects regardless. Our reasons for wanting windows are much the same as they have always been, except that today we want not only increased light but greater freedom, a sense of immediate contact with the outdoors, even if our outdoors is only a tiny urban patch. Enlightened basement conversions, with new glazed doors opening onto the garden, can only be an improvement on the damp underlit places basements were in the days when people had servants, who were contained literally 'below stairs'. But there are proprieties to be observed when making fundamental changes to buildings. The craze that overtook so many rural conversions in the fifties and sixties for replacing draughty wooden casements in timber framed cottages with doubled glazed metal framed windows, was a misguided application of modernisation which left many attractive old houses uneasily hybrid, neither one thing nor the other. New wooden framed windows, optionally double glazed, might have been a little more expensive, but they would have respected the character of the buildings and settled into their irregular fabric.

One cannot formulate any rules for this sort of exercise; only urge people to look at what they have, value it properly, and be imaginative about changing it. Be realistic too. There is no sense in throwing open a whole wall with a large picture

38

RIGHT: *A velvet draped baldacchino and groups of tall arched windows either side make a grand effect in this country bedroom belonging to writer Lisa St Aubin de Teran, where the splendid brass bed is set sensibly, but unexpectedly, on the diagonal.*

ABOVE: *A spectacular use of the grid makes a dramatic glazed chequerboard of one wall of a Californian room. Instead of one window there are thirty-six, all designed to open, and the effect of this overscaled grid plus its shadow partner on the floor is somehow more impressive, as well as more practical, than one huge sheet of glass. The view undoubtedly helps.*

window, or glazed doors, if you then feel paranoid about being spied on by the neighbours, or burgled the moment you leave the house, or forget that heat escapes through large expanses of glass and shiver all winter.

INSULATION

Double glazing is the standard answer to insulation these days, practical and effective when well done. Sealed units are generally reckoned to be the most efficient system, and they can be made up to fit any size or type of window. With other systems, especially do-it-yourself kits, there is a chance of condensation getting between the panes and misting over the glass. What double glazing really does most effectively is cut down on draughts. But, according to tests, properly lined and interlined curtains, drawn close at night, do this almost as effectively.

VENTILATION

An important function of windows, less publicised than it used to be in an age given over to air conditioning, is to ventilate rooms properly, so that stale air can be renewed and rooms smell fresh and sweet. Fresh air used to be thought of as a panacea for all minor ills, and domestic manuals in the early part of this century were full of instructions about keeping the windows open at night, and keeping an invalid's room properly aired. Fresh air, it was felt, would blow away the germs. Whether air blowing in off traffic laden streets is so fresh is debatable, but it remains true that rooms without easy access to the outside, like some hotel bedrooms, rapidly feel claustrophobic, especially in hot weather. Windows do not need to be large or wide open to keep a room aired; the main thing is to encourage a through draught between door and window. Where ventilation often does need boosting in a house is in the kitchen. Fans installed in the window glass are a help here, but not as effective as a fan in a hood over the cooking area, which draws smoke, steam and smells away at source.

——— ROOM WITH A VIEW ———

Windows should frame and make the most of an attractive view; yet it is surprising how many houses turn their backs on their best outlook. It may be that the landscape has changed since they were built, but often houses were built with their main rooms facing north to avoid sunlight which would fade carpets and covers. Today, we would rather have the sun and the faded colours.

Putting in a window, or glazed French windows, or both, can transform a room with a south or west facing aspect, making it feel years younger, so to speak, and a lot more joyful. Morning sunshine is a free tonic, and the best way to eat breakfast and prepare oneself for the day. If windows are to capitalise on a good view it is important to bring them down low enough so that you can look out while sitting down, or lying in bed if the view is from a bedroom. A simple alteration along these lines was spectacularly successful in the bedroom of a third floor flat overlooking leafy London gardens. By substituting French windows with a tiny balcony for the existing small window, its owner made the room feel much larger, let in a great deal more light and gave herself a green outlook from her bed, framed by potplants on her balcony. At night, an uplighter among the plants on the balcony gave a glamorous illusion of waving greenery, pretty impressive mileage from one tiny railed perch three floors up.

Greenery is not the only view worth enhancing. City lights, chimneypots, even grim industrial townscapes can be good to look out upon. Water is always fascinating, which is why houses near the sea and apartments on river banks are always sought after. Fantastic views need little elaboration in the framing. The round topped windows in a water tower Piers Gough recently converted into an enviable flat seven floors up above the Thames are simply draped in creamy cotton sheeting caught up at each side of the windows during the day and falling loose at night. Against walls of exposed brick, the sheeting looks luxurious enough, without being fussy or detracting from the spectacular views.

High windows are dramatic, especially in cities, and best of all at night. Americans, more accustomed to high living and wide panoramas, show great flair in decorating rooms with a view. Often the style is to play down the room with neutral colours and sophisticated textures, with intimate, shadowy, careful lighting, so that attention is captured by a huge uncurtained window framing the breathtaking dazzle of a big city lit up by night. If the sun beats in too fiercely windows like these

41

can be screened off either with rattan roller blinds inside, or awnings outside, both of which can be adjusted to let in as much light as one wants. Greenery is a good foil to a view. Ideally it should be big and bold and strongly shaped, a couple of tall ficus trees or citrus trees in tubs, not a row of little pot plants on the window sill.

In dire cases the view may need eliminating, where a window looks out into a dim light well full of air conditioning vents, or faces a dour building just across the way. Most places have one ill favoured window which needs screening. Depending on the size of the window, the amount of light you need from it, and whether you just want to soften the prospect or block it right out, there are lots of solutions which might apply. Clear glass can be replaced with frosted, or engraved, or prettily coloured glass, or a medley of these. This is handy

if you want to forget the view. A roller blind, stencilled with the sort of view you *would* like, is easily come by these days with so many young designers trying their hand at interior artwork.

——— GLASS BRICKS ———

With the great revival of interest in houses of the inter-war years, one use of glass looks about due for a come-back. Glass bricks, used with triumphant sophistication in houses like the Maison de Verre in Paris, have been downgraded in recent years to a purely functional role, letting in overhead light in basement areas, even public lavatories, anywhere that needed privacy and a light source that was also structurally tough. But when they are employed as they were in the Maison de Verre and other houses of the period, as a translucent wall or part of a wall, they are not simply functional but sleek and elegant. Properly used, glass bricks are enjoyably ambiguous – combining the solidity of bricks with the translucency of glass. A slice of wall filled in with glass bricks is poised visually somewhere between wall and window. This ambiguity allows, indeed invites, visual surprises. Some of the all-glass walls in the Maison de Verre surround small clear glass windows, so that translucency is played off against transparency as with some Lalique pieces. Alternatively, an entrance hall might have a solid wood or metal door set into a translucent wall of glass bricks, reversing our usual expectations. Design games like these make glass brick walls decorative and ideally suited to the smoothly detailed, pared down chic that accompanied the austere luxury of furniture by such designers as Eileen Gray and Mies van der Rohe. One very elegant Brussels house, designed in 1929 by the Belgian architect Louis de Koninck, combines glass brick exterior and internal walls with concrete columns, tubular metal handrails and superb thirties furniture and paintings; the result is an interior that sums up all that was best in the twenties and thirties style.

It would be a mistake to incorporate glass brick walls into a building opening onto magnificent views. There, the translucency would merely be teasing. But in densely built-up urban settings, where the outlook is nothing special, their translucency is a distinct bonus, giving an illusion of openness and freedom, with solid walls opened up

ABOVE: *Elegant minimalism in a bathroom designed by Eva Jiricna. Panels of marble have been cleverly used to obscure a large window with an unattractive outlook, leaving only one sleek steel porthole to admit a little light and ventilation.*

RIGHT: *A solid curve of glass bricks makes a glowing band of light in the otherwise traditional clapboard frontage of a house in Dallas, Texas. The curved translucent wall illustrates well the dramatic ambiguity of this newly fashionable material.*

WINDOWS

44

to the light and seasons, without any sacrifice of privacy. At night, when lit from within and seen from without, they suddenly turn into blocks of warm light set in a darkened façade.

Equally successful is the use of these blocks for internal walls. De Koninck set his in a painted grid of metal or wood for a crisper effect. Used as a translucent partition between lobby and central galleried room, it combines the precise lines of graph paper with something of the delicacy of oiled paper Japanese screens, and makes a splendid foil to leather and chrome furniture, deep pile rugs with abstract designs and doors of sleek red lacquer. Seeing houses of this period restored to their period decor is fascinating evidence of the inflexibility of their architectural style. Unlike many earlier period houses, which can accommodate an eclectic mix of furnishings and interior styles, these austere buildings are emasculated by any but authentic thirties furnishings. Flowered carpets, chintz, sets of prints, nests of tables, pretty table lamps – the merest suggestion of any of this sort of prettification makes them into uneasy travesties, stark as locker rooms instead of suave as a Cunard liner.

MAKING CHANGES

Putting in windows where there were none before can be a useful way of getting more light inside a house and may be essential if you are doing internal conversion work dividing large rooms or knocking two small ones into one. You may also need to add extra windows if you have bought an old property which was designed with few windows in order either to keep heat in or to avoid the dreaded window tax of the eighteenth century.

While planning and building regulations are laid down they may be interpreted differently depending on what part of the country you live in. So before setting to and knocking holes in your walls it is a good idea to get in touch with the planning authorities at your local town hall and check if what you intend to do to your home is acceptable to them. If you live in a designated conservation area of any kind there will probably be restrictions on the kind of windows – if any – that you can install. If your home is part of a terrace you may not be allowed to make any alterations which would affect the uniform look of the façades. And if you

45

LEFT: *With its beautifully detailed stacks of drawer, shelf and cupboard units converging on an elegant arched window, this scheme shows what original results can be achieved with a dormer window in an attic room.*

are planning to fit windows in your home which would mean that your neighbours' properties are overlooked you will probably need to get written agreement from them before the planning authorities give you the go-ahead. Do not skip this stage when improving your home as the authority has the right to insist that you restore the property to its original state if you instal windows where permission would have been refused.

If you can't get permission to fit a window where you want a new one you could consider painting a trompe l'oeil one on an inside wall, either doing it yourself if you have the talent or employing a mural artist to paint one for you. Trompe l'oeil windows offer a lot of design scope in terms of what view you decide to show through them and can be used to good effect to adjust the proportions of a room where you feel an extra window would add more character than simply hanging a picture. And, of course, a trompe l'oeil window can be dressed in the same way as any other window with curtains or a blind.

Once you have established that you can make new windows it is worth consulting an architect or structural engineer to ensure that the size and the materials you plan to use are suitable and that creating new windows will not cause problems with the main structure of the building. You may also need professional help with designing the windows to ensure that they are constructed in a way which is safe and does not interfere with the load-bearing qualities of the walls.

Window frames wear out well before the rest of the fabric of a house and need to be replaced. Technological developments have meant that you do not need to replace wood with wood but can choose also between upvc, aluminium and steel. Again, it is essential to consider the appearance of the windows; many homes have been ruined by the indiscriminate replacement of traditional wood frames by poorly designed metal ones. At the cheaper end of the market replacement windows come in standard designs which may not be suitable for your home. You might do well to pay more and go for custom-made designs which will enhance the appearance both inside and out.

If you are having your windows replaced, this is the time to consider whether to double glaze them. Even if you decide to stick with single glazing the same rules apply for finding an installer. Choose

one who is reputable and likely to stay in business since replacing windows can produce problems and you may find that a spell of bad weather reveals gaps or draughts that you will want the original installer to put right.

With new or replacement windows it is worth spending some time deciding how you want them to open and close. There are various hinges and tilting mechanisms on the market which give more flexibility than windows had originally. You can eliminate prevailing winds by opening some windows in a particular direction and also make them easier to clean by fitting windows which can be turned round to allow you to reach both sides.

Simple alterations can change the effect of a window's shape without requiring major structural work. For example, fixing curved pieces of wood at the top interior of windows can produce an arched effect which could reflect arches used in the decor of a room. Leading can be laid over windows to produce a leaded light or other design of panes.

SECURITY PROBLEMS

As crime increases it becomes ever more essential to fit security devices to windows. Although a really determined burglar is not put off by them, police claim that the casual thief is deterred by the extra time required to break through a window which has special locks. Fitting security devices does not mean your home has to be hermetically sealed each time you go out. You can fit the type of lock which allows you to leave windows slightly ajar but unable to be opened any further without using the key. Because windows vary so much in size, shape and the way they open it is impossible to be specific about the best type of lock to fit. The Crime Prevention Officer from your local police station or a reputable locksmith should be able to advise you on the most suitable type.

For wooden framed windows there is a wide choice of locks for casement, sash and sliding openings and most can be fitted by anyone who is reasonably competent at DIY. For metal framed windows the locks are more difficult to fit and unless you are sure you can cope it is probably best to have them fitted professionally. This is essential with aluminium framed windows because of the design and construction of the frames. Louvre windows are very popular with burglars as they are

RIGHT: *Security devices need not look grim. With its wrought iron filigree painted white, like lace, and a surround of flourishing greenery, this little window looks deceptively inviting. But the iron bars are for real.*

ABOVE: *From North Africa via Spain, this handsome cage of decorative ironwork in a surround of blue and white tiles adds dignity as well as security to an old house in Lima, Peru.*

easy to force and often the glass panels can be lifted out from the outside. To secure them, either glue the glass panels to the end sections and fit steel bars over them or fit one of the louvres which is specially designed to be secure.

If you live in a high-risk area where burglary is a common occurrence you may decide to fit window grilles or shutters to prevent glass being broken. Before doing so, you should take professional advice as there are safety implications: you might not be able to escape if there was a fire or other hazard. Grilles and shutters are usually custom made to fit your windows, so there is no reason why they should not be an attractive additional feature of the windows rather than the prison-like bars or unimaginative grilles which so many people put up with. Roller shutters may be fitted inside or outside the panes and in addition to security offer some degree of heat insulation and also cut noise levels from outside.

——— DECORATIVE TREATMENT ———

It is important not to make snap decisions about how to deal with windows when you move into or build a new home. You need to live with them for a time in order to find out how the light falls – or fails to fall – into each room at different times of day and also work out which times of day and evening you spend in each room. If you need privacy while working out your decor just tack an old sheet or rug along the top of the window at night.

The view from your window will obviously be a major factor in deciding how you treat it. If it is an attractive one you will want to see as much of it as possible and may prefer to fit a blind rather than curtains so that it gets as much exposure as possible. If it is a dull or ugly view you will want to hide it, perhaps with nets or a blind over the window and curtains at either side. You could even adopt an extreme solution and block out the view completely with a false wall or painted glass.

There is also the question of the window surround. In older and some well-designed modern houses the window frame may be a thing of beauty in itself or have the kind of ornamental shutters which it would be a crime to cover up. Or the window frame may be fairly ordinary but the surrounding area empty enough to be decorated with stencils or a decorative paint finish. In this case you may only need a simple blind, but there is no need at all for window dressings if the frame itself is attractive and/or the glass in it ornamental. Unless you actually need darkness in a room because it is slept in, it can be a pleasure to watch twilight descend over an attractive view.

Most traditional windows have some form of surround, though this may be no more than a plastered reveal. There is a problem involved in positioning a window in a wall which arises simply from the disparity in thickness between a solid wall and a window frame. The simplest window is merely a glass equivalent of the stone slab once used to block 'wind eyes'. Where the walls are a couple of feet thick, as they often are in old buildings, the window seems to be set at the mouth of a deep hole scooped in the wall. In some cases these are merely plastered over to smooth the surface, but usually the hole is boxed in with wood to give a finished look, and to make dusting and cleaning easier.

Until the Georgian era windows were set flush with the external walls, with some form of 'dripstone' arrangement above to direct rain off the window surface down the walls. This usually left a deep embrasure on the interior wall, and the way these were handled is very much a period feature. The recess could simply be finished continuously with the walls or, more usefully and attractively, fitted with a seat. Window seats are found in Tudor and Jacobean houses. By the early eighteenth century shutters were a normal feature, often folding back into a wooden box frame with a deep window seat fitted between the shutter boxes. As windows began to be set back from the exterior walls, in Georgian buildings, the recesses grew shallower internally. Window seats disappeared and shutter boxes tended to be set at an angle. By the 1830s the wooden surrounds had become conspicuous features of a room, wide and handsomely constructed, with panelled shutters and wide architraves. The succession of shallow planes, interrupted by mouldings, sets off the window and gives importance to it much as a good picture frame does to a painting. By this time curtains were a standard part of a room's furnishings, and these wide surrounds allowed them to be looped back on either side during the day without blocking much light from the window itself. Also, because of the shallowness of the surrounds, the curtains did not stand out into the room space, but merged almost continuously with the wall surface, which looked tidy and spacious.

Victorian windows ranged in style from neo-medieval oriels like the one at William Morris's Red House, to the apres Queen Anne window seated type favoured by Norman Shaw, taking in a lively variety of alternatives along the way. Perhaps the characteristic Victorian window is the three sided bay window, to be seen on houses all the way up the social scale. The larger versions achieve a certain grandeur, and were large enough to form a space which could be furnished with a table, books and a few chairs, to take advantage of the concentrated light they gave. But the smaller, shallow copies seen on so many genteel little Victorian villas present a problem to their present owners, too shallow to take a window seat, draughty and expensive to curtain. Victorian joinery however, was invariably solid and workmanlike, and windows of this period are properly framed. It was not till after World War I that the Modern window, often metal framed and set in a simple plastered reveal with perhaps a narrow wooden sill, became standard in new buildings. Wide and shallow, with the sills set relatively high to the overall height of the rooms, these are difficult to deal with unless you happen to like the

SURROUNDS

"There was King Bradmond's palace,
Was never none richer, the story says;
For all the windows and the walls
Were painted with gold, both towers
and halls;
Pillars and doors all were of brass;
Windows of latten were set with glass;
It was so rich, in many wise,
That it was like a paradise.

Sir Bevis of Hampton (c. 1325)
Author unknown

50

RIGHT: *A little nothing of a window, a small casement without the usual wooden frame, is raised to new status with a cunning use of paint. We sprayed stencilled designs above and below to 'open up' the window in relation to the wall, and painted a frame all round.*

51

slightly stark effect of Venetian blinds hung just inside or outside the reveal. A typically contemporary window, like a typical contemporary painting, often has no frame at all; it is simply a slice of wall which has become glass and can be opened out.

TREATMENTS FOR SURROUNDS

Nicely-made wooden surrounds are usually, and sensibly, painted in pale light-reflecting colours to blend with the wall finishes. Where the idea is to maximise any light, as with a small deep-set cottage window, shiny or mid-sheen white paint is the traditional finish. It is easy to keep clean, looks neat and fresh, and makes a good display of a potted plant. The more elaborate joinery that made up the wooden window frames, boxed or splayed, of larger houses, often panelled out with mouldings, can take more intense decorative treatments. Where the pine used is good quality, straight grained and warm toned, stripping and waxing gives a mellow looking frame to a window, needing no maintenance and making curtains unnecessary. Windows like these are very much a room feature, and people often like to stress their scale and dignity with a combination of paint finishes. Simple dragging, in various tones of off-white (darkest tone inside the panels, middle tone for mouldings, palest for the surround) underlines their three dimensional quality without fuss. Or the same idea can be carried out in a colour related to the room colours; painting the surrounds to

53

LEFT: *Designer craftsman Richard La Trobe Bateman replaced the sash windows in his 1715 stone house with simple elm-framed casements in the same vernacular style and spirit as the furniture he made to stand in it.*

ABOVE: *The joinery which went into the making of window surrounds in the early nineteenth century was of the highest order. The artist who lives here decided to strip the wood down to its knotless pine and let the proportions and detailing speak for themselves.*

continue the wall colour makes them look less dramatic but can give the room itself more coherence. For instance, in a small study used mostly at night, incoming light may be less important than the restfulness of one good colour used positively throughout.

Where the windows are going to be curtained, there is not much point overplaying the decorative effects on the surrounds. On the other hand there is a case for leaving the elegance of some windows untramelled, with perhaps a simple roller or festoon blind to filter the light or screen the window at night, and this is where decoration can make a lot of impact. The recessed panelling on old shutter boxes, and beneath windows, seems to invite something interesting within the 'frames'. At Charleston, Vanessa Bell and Duncan Grant used them like pictures, gleefully painting them up in their own light, decorative style, in glowing colours. More formally, there are examples where the panels were filled in with intricate stencilled 'marquetry', in woody shades of buff to tawny brown, with the rest of the surrounds being wood grained in a soft golden brown. Matching the door treatments, these look rich and surprising, and very grand. Marquetry patterns are not too difficult to come by – you can take a tracing of an actual piece, or get a photograph blown up to size, though many designs may need to be tinkered about with to make them long and narrow enough to fit. Each shade in the final pattern needs a different stencil cut for it, and acrylic colours or signwriter's paints are both suitable paints for stencilling, thin textured and fast drying. If you are not up to wood graining, simply dragging the flat areas in a woody tinted glaze over cream or buff will give a woody effect easily. The mouldings should be picked out separately in a darker brown, or black, for emphasis. Any lavish decoration like this needs to be varnished over to protect it; the professionals prefer a matt or low sheen effect, which you can get by mixing gloss and matt varnishes, or by applying a gloss varnish and abrading the surface with cabinet paper or soft wire wool to dull it down.

Really superb joinery can take a palatial treatment such as Chinoiserie decoration. Here the finish is shiny, because the idea is to imitate old lacquer. A simplified version, using deep rich colours, with the mouldings picked out in a colour

55

LEFT: *Chinoiserie decoration, that playfully exotic style which reached Europe from the East in the late seventeenth century, was the ideal treatment for parts of this little pleasure house, the Pagodenburg Pavilion, built by Joseph Effner for the Elector Max Emanuel in the grounds of the Nymphenburg Palace.*

or gold transfer leaf, would still look handsome. Chinoiserie stencils are now available, too, which can be grouped in various ways to fill the panels. Consult old lacquered screens for colour suggestions. The stencilling could be done in Humbrol enamels or spray paints, but the final deep gloss is best arrived at by repeated coats of thinned varnish, applied overall and rubbed down gently; bandbox newness, a slick gloss overall, is wrong where you are aiming for something charmingly aged looking.

If all this sounds like hard work, there is a simpler way of adding lustre to panelled surrounds and/or shutterboxes, which Sir John Soane used in his extraordinary house in Lincoln's Inn, now a museum. This is to introduce mirror glass. Soane used mirrors in all sorts of ingenious ways, both to reflect more light and to create illusions. Mirrors set inside the panels would do both, very effectively. I would use the dark, slightly clouded mirror glass with an antique finish which most

glaziers stock, have the pieces cut to fit exactly and glue them in place.

So far we have only considered windows with traditional timber surrounds. Where these are lacking, windows are apt to look a little stark and unfinished. In some cases it may be possible to get a wooden surround installed, or at least a wooden sill, without removing the window itself or preventing it from opening. Where this is either impossible, or too expensive, painted illusions can help. Windows on the Continent are often 'framed', outside and inside, with wide painted bands in a contrasting colour, which is a simple way of making them more important. This suits any rustic looking building. A prettier, softer way of framing a window would be to stencil a decorative border all the way round, preferably matching a border elsewhere in the room. You could stencil some of the motifs from the border on a roller blind, using fabric paints. This would look best on a square or rectangular, rather than horizontal

57

LEFT: *Naive floral stencils were used to introduce colour and outline the generous width of window in this fine beamed kitchen in John and Gabrielle Sutcliffe's eighteenth century Norfolk farmhouse.*

ABOVE: *With yards of silvery photographic material, dozens of silk red roses and lots of bravura, Jon Lys Turner has made something dreamlike and surreal from this plain window looking onto an undistinguished London garden.*

window. Another painted effect flattering to windows set well below the ceiling line is to use the space above the window to paint an arrangement of swags and bows. This could be lightheartedly classical, with thick ropes of fruit, flowers and leaves looped from a central motif such as a bow, cupid or ram's head, caught up at the corners, above the window, and then falling in fat pendants on either side. More simply, it could show painted draperies, falling from ribbon bows. For inspiration consult old pattern books, such as *The Cabinet Maker's Drawing Book* by Sheraton or *The Architect's Storehouse*, by Robert Pricke, first published in 1674, and available now in facsimile.

Horizontal or 'picture' windows, are less tractable, at least to painted decoration. Their proportions are too uncompromisingly modern for painted frippery and simple painted bands would emphasize their horizontality too much. Two possibilities are worth looking into, however. The simplest is to face the window reveal, usually simply plastered, with mirror glass, either cut to fit and screwed in place, or simply bought in flexible sheets of tiny squares, cut and glued. Alternatively, windows like these can be incorporated into a wall of shelving, or cupboards, or both. Window walls tend to be overlooked, though the natural lighting could make a feature like this practical as well as substantial looking. It is the flimsiness, apparent rather than real, which makes many of these perfunctorily finished picture windows look unsympathetic – framing them with shelves of books, hi-fi equipment, plants, etc, is a nice way of humanising them visually, and as practical as any exponent of Modernism could wish. A continuous shelf under the window substitutes for a sill, and the sheer bulk of books or records is quite a useful muffler of sounds from outside, an acoustic bonus.

DECORATIVE PAINT FINISHES

You can make a window frame a really spectacular part of a room's decor by applying a decorative paint finish to it. Wooden window frames are the easiest to do but it is also possible to apply these finishes to metal provided it is first well primed. Upvc frames cannot be decorated in this way.

First wash the frame all over and thoroughly with a solution of water and sugar soap made up according to the manufacturer's instructions.

Allow it to dry completely. In the case of wood, sand it well so that the surface is as smooth as possible. Use the tool of a vacuum cleaner to make sure that you clear up all traces of the sanding so that it won't spoil the paint surface. Now apply knotting to all the knots in the wood. (Knotting is a special sealant designed to ensure that nothing exudes from the knots in wood to spoil the paint.) Sand the wood well again and once more clear up all traces of the sanding. Apply a coat of wood primer (metal primer on metal) at this stage. This will show up any irregularities in the wooden frames which should be filled, using a proprietary product. Allow the filling to dry completely and sand the frame again.

Apply the first coat of the base colour, fairly thinly. Sand the frame again and apply a second coat of the base colour. Check the window frame and make sure that you have an absolutely smooth perfect surface. If not, continue to sand and apply base coat until you have. If you skip stages or start to decorate on a less than perfect base you will not achieve a good special effect when you have applied the next treatment.

Specialist paint finishes consist of two layers of paint or glaze and the interaction between the base and top coat. You can use either oil-based or water-based paint but must not mix the two. An oil-based paint will wear better than a water-based one but takes considerably longer to dry when applied. Oil-based paint does not need a coating of protective varnish; water-based paint usually does if it is not to be marked by fingers and the possible rubbing of curtains or blinds. If you are using water-based paint and intend to apply a protective seal remember that it will slightly alter the effect and colour of your finish. You can apply a matt, satin or gloss finish but all will tend to yellow with time. Choose an interior polyurethane varnish, bearing in mind that it must be labelled 'clear' on the tin. Matt is easier to apply than a gloss finish and also has a less noticeable effect on the finish.

PAINT TERMINOLOGY

Colour wash can be made up from emulsion paint mixed with water. It can also be made from raw colour or gouache mixed with water and a little unibond for adhesion.

Oil glaze consists of transparent oil glaze (also known as scumble glaze) mixed with white spirit, a

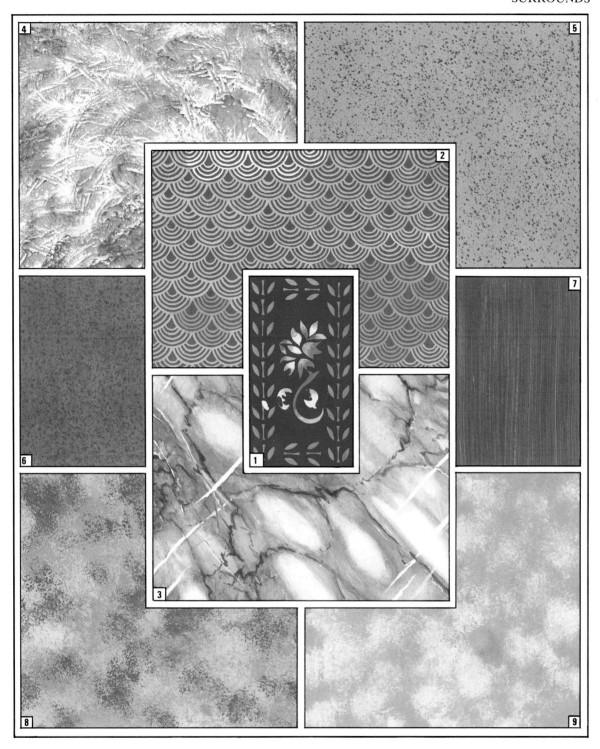

ABOVE: *A selection of special paint effects. (1) Stencilled (2) Combed (3) Marbled (4) Ragged (5) Spattered (6) Stippled (7) Dragged (8) Sponging on (9) Sponging off.*

little undercoat and tinting colour (artists' oils or universal stainer).

Spirit glaze is standard eggshell paint thinned with white spirit.

SPONGED ON EFFECT

Use either oil glaze or vinyl silk emulsion thinned with water to the desired colour. You will need a frilly natural sponge, small enough to fit comfortably in your hand, and a rag or piece of card to wipe off excess paint from the sponge.

Dip the sponge into the thinned mixture and remove all excess. Check that you have the right amount of paint on it by testing on a piece of blank paper. Then dab it over the window surround, creating a random pattern and turning the sponge with each dab so that you don't get a potato print or lino cut effect. When you have covered the whole window frame, stand back from it and screw up your eyes so you can check the light and dark areas and fill in where you have missed. If necessary, you can tape a small piece of sponge to a cane and use it to fill in small areas which are difficult to reach.

If you accidentally oversponge an area and create a mark, leave it until it is dry. Take a tiny piece of sponge and pick it through with the base coat colour to even up the pattern.

SPONGED OFF EFFECT

Mix your glaze to the desired colour and select a frilly sponge as for sponging on. For this effect you need plenty of time and no interruptions. When doing a large area such as a wall two people are needed, but you can sponge a window frame on your own provided you work quickly so the glaze does not dry before you have sponged off.

Apply the glaze to one complete section of the window frame, then take the sponge and dab over it to create the pattern. Work in the same way as for sponging on, turning the sponge with each dab unless you want a repetitive pattern, and take care not to press too hard. This effect is difficult to correct, so take care not to brush against it while it is drying.

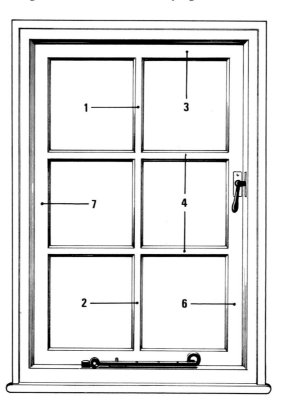

DRAGGED EFFECT

Dragging is a more difficult and demanding technique than sponging on or off and if a window frame is to be your first attempt it is a good idea to practise beforehand on a piece of vertical card or timber.

Use oil glaze, tinted to the desired colour. You will need an ordinary brush to apply the glaze and for the dragging a worn down cheap brush with sparse, stubbly bristles is useful. Like sponging off, this is a technique which on large areas normally requires two people.

With wooden frames you should always drag in the direction of the grain. Because dragging can result in a build up of paint at the bottom of the drag it is essential to divide the frame into vertical and horizontal sections and to do each one separately. If you are deft there is no need to wait until one section is dry before beginning the next.

The illustration shows the order in which to drag a basic window frame. Use it as a guideline to work out how to do more complex frames. Unless you are very neat it is a good idea to mask the window glass and wall while you are working.

Apply the mixed glaze to each section in turn and draw the brush down it. To avoid 'curtaining' (the wavy effect that you can get at the top of a drag) start the dragging movement before you

ABOVE: *Drag a window in this order, if possible waiting until each section is dry before you drag the one next to it. Try to execute the drags with bold sweeps of the brush and avoid a messy touched up area where sections meet.*

actually touch the glaze. With window frames you should be able to complete each drag in one movement. It is essential to wipe the brush after each drag before starting again at the top. To prevent a build-up of paint at the bottom of each drag, try to reduce the pressure as you move down the stroke. Keep a small paint brush handy for correcting any drag which has gone crooked.

COMBED EFFECT

Combing as a technique is really more suitable for larger, flatter areas than window frames. But if you are prepared to practise or want a particular combed effect there is no reason why it should not be done successfully. You will need a graining comb (available from art shops) which is made from steel, is flexible and can be held in a flame to clean when clogged up.

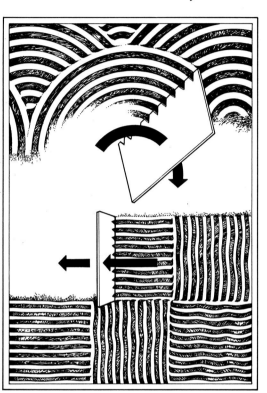

Use an oil glaze of a thicker consistency than for the previous techniques, so add more undercoat or an oil based paint such as alkyd semigloss to the basic oil glaze. Apply the glaze section by section before starting to comb.

Combing is a technique which offers a lot of scope for experiment. You can create geometric or abstract designs and indeed imitate fabric warp and weft. By turning the comb as in the illustration you can produce basketwork or shell designs. Practise on thin card the width of your window frame to see what design would be more suitable and also be possible to do, bearing in mind the curves and grooves on your particular frame.

STIPPLED EFFECT

For this you need tinted oil glaze and a stippling brush or decorator's pure bristle dusting brush. Apply the glaze a section at a time, then bounce the brush over the wet surface of the frame to create a soft, powdery effect. The finish produced is subtle and can be as dense as you please. Allow the stippled finish to dry thoroughly in an even temperature to avoid bloom appearing on the stippled surface.

RAGGED EFFECT

For this you need a basic oil glaze and a supply of old rags which should all be of the same fabric. Absorbent materials will produce a softer effect than less absorbent ones. This finish can also be achieved by using rolled up plastic sheeting. When you have finished ragging you will have a lot of stained, dirty rag bundles which should not be burned or put in a bin as they are highly combustible. Dispose of them at the local authority dump.

Apply the glaze a section at a time, then bunch up a rag in your hand so it presents a compact surface with as many creases as possible. Dab this over the glazed area, altering the prints by changing the shape of the rag or the direction.

SPATTERED EFFECT

This type of finish can be very effective but may be considered rather labour-intensive for a window frame. It is particularly messy to carry out, so mask off the surrounding walls, floors and furnishings, including the window glass. The glaze should neither be too runny, in which case it will form drips and a rain spattered effect, nor too stiff, in which case it will not come easily off the brush. Use a brush with short, stiff bristles; a toothbrush is a good choice for a window frame.

Dip the brush in the glaze and, holding it still at right angles to the surface, use your thumb to flick

61

ABOVE: *On flat window surrounds use a comb to create your own patterns. For the chequer board effect execute horizontal and vertical strokes alternately. A clamshell effect can be produced by turning the comb with each stroke; start at the bottom of the design and work upwards.*

down sharply on the bristles. With a little practice the glaze can be directed accurately. Practise first for accuracy and distance with a piece of card.

MARBLED EFFECT

Marbling is a specialised technique that really needs practice. If you want a truly professional finish it is probably best to employ an expert rather than do it yourself. However, if you want to try it, this is how it is done.

The surface should be painted in a colour to match the ground tint of your chosen marble. You will need a selection of artists' brushes for applying colour and veining and a painter's dust brush for softening. Study a piece of real marble. To achieve the same effect, brush veins in shakily, like roads on a map. To soften, move the dust brush gently over the veins to blur them slightly. Paint in 'pebbles' with a larger brush. Soften the whole surface by dabbing with soft paper. Highlights or

dark veins can be put in with a fine sable and more variety can be achieved by flicking a little white spirit here and there. When dry, varnish well.

—— STENCILLING ——

For this you need stencil board, obtainable from artist's suppliers. Alternatively, thin card can be coated with shellac or varnish to prevent the paint soaking into it. Plan your design, trace it onto the stencil board and cut it out with a sharp craft knife. If you are not good at creating your own design you can trace one from a book or a pattern that you like. You can also buy ready-cut stencil kits in a range of designs. For stencilling, mix up your second colour with white emulsion and acrylics. Keep the mixture fairly stiff as you will be working mainly in the vertical plane and you don't want it to drip. If you want to create a two-colour design you will need to cut two stencils.

62

ABOVE: *You can do away with curtains altogether and make the backs of shutters as attractive as the fronts when they are prettily stencilled. Hand Painted Stencils, the partnership of Felicity Binyon and Elizabeth MacFarlane, did these for a small London dining room.*

A light spray of spray adhesive will hold your stencil to the wall, or use masking tape to hold it down. It should be removed as soon as you have completed stencilling. Take up *very* little colour on your brush. Test on spare paper, then dab firmly with the stencil brush, keeping it at right angles to the stencil so that you don't get dragged lines. Put the brush down and remove the stencil carefully, taking care not to smudge the edges of the design.

FABRIC SURROUND

A fabric-covered surround gives a window frame harmony with its window dressing and is fairly easy to do. It is also a good way of disguising an ugly frame or one which is in poor condition. You will need to do a test to see if a latex adhesive will show through the fabric you have chosen. Although latex adhesive, which is white and flexible, dries to a transparent film, it may show through a light

coloured fabric and give it a stained appearance. If this is the case you will have to cut thick card or thin ply to the size and shape to be covered and stick the fabric round it so that the adhesive is on the back of the card or ply and won't show through. Keep the covered panels in position using either a contact or epoxy resin adhesive or panel pins. If the fabric is one which is likely to fray, either overcast the edges before sticking, apply an anti-fray spray or use plenty of adhesive so that all the edges of the fabric are well covered. You could also use braid to edge the fabric.

WINDOW FRAMES

The material that a window frame is made from will affect its life and performance while in use. Modern materials such as steel and upvc offer some advantages over traditional wood and are sometimes worth considering if you are building a

63

ABOVE: *Nothing looks cosier than fabric, but windows this size would cost a fortune to curtain. Fabric, glued and stapled around the entire window area, gives an impression of curtained cosiness at a fraction of the cost.*

home from scratch or if you are replacing existing windows because they are worn out or because you want to alter their style.

Wood is the original material used for windows and if you want to have a timber effect you need to use the real thing. Fortunately, manufacturers of other window frame materials have steered clear of the 'wood effect' which appears so disastrously on furniture and interior fitments. To support effectively, timber used for window frames must be a hardwood; this tends to be very expensive because of its slow growth and the need for seasoning to prevent warping. But even the best hardwood has a shorter life than many man-made materials and needs more maintenance. Wood is affected by weather both dry and wet and has a tendency to warp as well as rot. So, although it may seem the obvious choice, it could be worth considering another material, even in the type of home which traditionally has wooden windows.

Metal windows may be aluminium or steel and have, in some people's minds, a tarnished image due to the tatty, unaesthetic examples which were installed when the materials were first used. Today's metal windows can be made to any shape, size and design and are cheaper, longer lasting and less in need of maintenance than wooden frames. Good quality metal frames receive a factory coating which resists rot and corrosion and can then be painted in the colour of your choice. You can also, with some brands, choose to have the inside and outside of the window frames painted in different colours.

Upvc window frames need even less maintenance than metal ones because you don't need to paint them. It is a good solid material that won't rot, warp or discolour and is good at insulating and minimising condensation. However, colour choice is more limited than with metal since upvc is self-coloured all the way through and is thus made in only a small range of colours.

CARE AND MAINTENANCE
Most window frames require some form of care and maintenance to keep them in good condition. The best time to deal with this is in the summer, before the winter weather damages them.

Metal frames require little attention. Aluminium is virtually maintenance free but some steel will show signs of rust. This should be removed by rubbing briskly with a wire brush, steel wool or emery cloth. Wear tough gloves and goggles to protect your eyes from flying particles. When the surface is clean, brush on a chemical rust remover and remove it according to the manufacturer's instructions with either water or spirit. Leave the frames to dry completely before applying a coat of metal primer followed by fresh paint. If you acquire a house where metal windows have been badly neglected and become very rusty you will need to replace them.

Upvc windows need no maintenance apart from

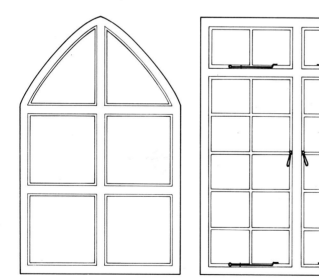
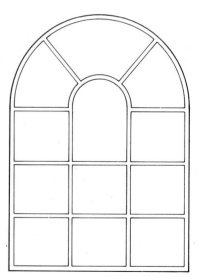

ABOVE: *The shape of a window may well dictate how you decide to dress it in terms of curtains or blinds. Where a frame is attractive you may want to leave it exposed, perhaps with a decorative paint finish*

ABOVE: *Surrounding a small window with mirror glass has turned this small alcove into a dressing table/boudoir right out of Dallas, swagged and bowed in pink silk and softly lit.*

a good brush from time to time to remove the dirt and dust that clings to the frames. Use a soft brush or cloth.

Wooden window frames tend to develop wet rot. To avoid this you should rub them down and apply a good sealant each year. Marine varnish or another tough outdoor seal is best. If the frames have become rotten you may be able to stop the rot by cutting the affected areas out completely, making sure you are into good wood by the time you have finished. Apply wood preservative to the cut surfaces and then insert new timber, cut to size and pre-treated. Badly rotted wooden frames will need to be replaced.

Check windows regularly to ensure that they are in good working condition, especially those which are not opened frequently. You may need to take some of the following remedial actions if they become stiff or jammed.

Wooden frame windows may stick if the wood has become wet and swollen. Plane down the whole side, or just over a small area if this is where the sticking occurs, but take care not to remove so much wood that the window lets in draughts. Apply primer to the planed surface and then paint or seal. If the frame is badly warped you will need to replace it.

Some windows stick because they have been clogged up with paint which was either not properly dry when the window was closed or which has been softened by sun beating on it. Use a chemical paint stripper to remove the layers of paint. This is a laborious job which may need to be undertaken in several stages. You may need to apply the paint stripper on the end of a scraper and work your way gradually across the frame. When the frame is clear of paint along the sticking areas apply the appropriate wood or metal primer and repaint.

REPLACING A SASH CORD

Sash cords need to be replaced at intervals; they either break because the window is opened and shut a lot or gently rot away because they are never moved. It is a fiddly job replacing them and one that tends to cost a lot of money if you call in a professional, so it's well worth taking the trouble to learn how to do it yourself. Don't attempt to do the job single handed. Sash windows are heavy when removed from their frames.

To renew the sash cord on a lower frame, start   67

LEFT: *All over tiling has always been popular in Continental kitchens because tiles are tough, practical and good looking. These handsome old tiles have their own patterned border and blue and white motifs in the style of old Delft. No need for any window treatment with these highly decorative walls.*

by removing the strips of beading using a blunt chisel. With your helper, lift the window a couple of inches and pull it forward so it comes away from its frame. Rest the side with the broken cord on a pair of steps, table or other solid object. Now remove the strip of timber which covers the weight compartment in the bottom of the frame and take out the weight. Pull out the broken pieces of cord and measure their total length. Cut the new cord to that length and fix one end of it to the weight, using the same method of attachment as the piece of cord you took off. Tie a short length of flexible weighting (a junk necklace or piece of curtain weight) to a long piece of string and – weight first – lower it into the casing over the pulley until you

can see it at the bottom. Tie the loose end of the string to something so that it doesn't get pulled down into the casing and remove the weight from the other end. To this end tie the new sash cord securely and use the other end of the string to pull the cord up the casing and over the pulley. Fix the weight back into its housing and secure the cord in its groove in the same way as the original cord. Lift the window back into position and check the movement by sliding it up and down to make sure the cord is the right length. Replace the strip of timber over the weight compartment and refix the strips of beading.

To replace the sash cord on a top window follow the same procedure but first remove the lower sash

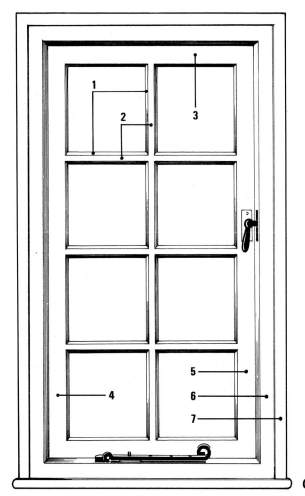

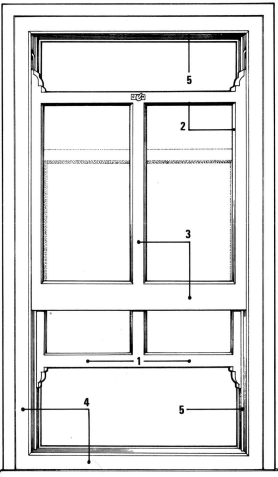

ABOVE: *Follow these sequences for painting casement and sash windows to gain the best results. Take care to finish off each paint stroke so that drips don't spoil the effect. Remove any masking tape from the glass as soon as you have finished.*

from its frame so that you can take out the parting beading between the two windows and swing the top window out.

PAINTING WINDOW FRAMES

Unless you have a painting hand that is as steady as a rock you are unlikely to be able to paint a window frame without marking the glass. To prevent this, fix masking tape around the edge of the pane, but do not leave it on any longer than necessary or it becomes difficult to remove. Apply it just before you start painting and remove it as soon as you finish. Ideally, you should paint windows first thing in the morning as this gives the paint enough time to dry before they need to be closed at night. Try not to get paint on window fittings and wipe them

over thoroughly when you have finished. Remove paint splashes from sash cords as soon as they occur; if you let the paint dry the cord will not run freely. When painting sash and casement windows follow the numerical sequence in the artwork illustrations opposite.

DRAUGHTPROOFING WINDOWS

You may find, particularly if you live in an exposed part of the country, that gaps appear between frame and glass and round the edges of your window frames between them and the brickwork. Either fill these with a patent sealing compound applied through a nozzle so that you can reach right into the gaps or fit water-resistant weather strips around the exterior of the frames.

70

The history of windows is intimately connected to the development of that mysterious, fragile, obdurate material called glass. Anyone who has pottered around archaeological exhibits knows that glass itself is an ancient discovery. It can be traced back 6000 years and vessels of glass, cloudy, opalescent and softly rounded, date back many centuries before Christ. By Roman times, the use of glass for glazing windows was well established. Pliny the Younger describes the 'beautifully designed alcove' in his villa, "which can be thrown into the room by folding back its glass doors. . . ." According to F. Palmer Cooke's lively book *Talk to me of Windows*, the first glazed windows date back to Imperial Rome. A swivelling glass circular pane found near the Forum at Pompeii is dated 60 BC, while in a villa on the Herculaneum Road a larger and more sophisticated window was discovered, with thick greenish glass panes held in lead cames like a Tudor casement.

If glazed windows were desirable in Italy, they must have seemed essential in northerly Roman Britain. Glass foundries have been excavated at Glastonbury, and near Norwich. But when the practical Romans withdrew from Britain their glazing techniques, along with other comforts like plumbing and heating, went with them. Except in a few ecclesiastical buildings, glazing was not seen again in Britain for over a thousand years.

Glass making was more advanced on the Continent, and it seems to have been French glaziers, probably accompanying the teams of master masons employed in church building, who put in the first coloured glass windows, amidst general wonder and amazement, in the thirteenth century.

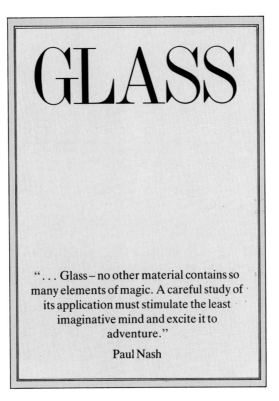

GLASS

" . . . Glass – no other material contains so many elements of magic. A careful study of its application must stimulate the least imaginative mind and excite it to adventure."

Paul Nash

France, but particularly Lorraine, was a great centre for glass making. The first recorded glazier to work in Britain was one Laurence Vitrearius ('glass man' in Latin) who arrived in Surrey from Normandy in 1226, and is known to have made clear and coloured glass for Westminster Abbey.

At first, glass was a luxury material, as can be seen from the fact that its use was reserved for churches, palaces and the homes of the nobility. So precious were glazed windows that they were designed to be detachable and transported from one patrician great house to another, when the family moved from their country estate to London, or vice versa. How the same window could fit two separately constructed apertures has not been recorded – perhaps this was one of the first instances of standardisation.

By Elizabeth's reign, accelerated by the influx of Huguenot refugees and glass workers from Lorraine, glazing was widespread enough to find its way into lesser homes. But the poor had to make do with wooden shutters or panes of horn, mica or oiled cloth for many centuries to come. The constant light that glazing provided was sufficiently novel and luxurious for Tudor building design to make a great parade of windows. The most celebrated example of conspicuous glazing is Hardwick Hall, the astonishing prodigy house built by the no less astonishing Bess of Hardwick when in her seventies, by which time she had survived four husbands, but still had enough energy to raise one of the most remarkable examples of the English vernacular style, in a commanding position on a hill in remote Derbyshire.

Sash windows, first used by Inigo Jones at Raynham Hall in 1630 and in common use by the

71

LEFT: *Bevelled glass glints and sparkles in an iron frame amid the decorative tracery of this modern stone window in the Middle East.*

mid-eighteenth century, revolutionised the appearance of windows, with their regular proportions and delicate grid of glazing bars. Interestingly, however, glass technology scarcely advanced for the next century or so. Georgian windows still used 'crown' or blown glass, cut from flattened discs or unrolled cylinders of mouth-blown glass. When glass production made a leap forward during the latter part of the nineteenth century and large, cheap sheets of glass started to be produced by the 'float' method, the way was open for architecture to change profoundly, for better and worse, during the next hundred years.

—— FUTURE GLASS TECHNOLOGY ——

The newest developments in glass technology have always been first adopted by the rich and powerful, then slowly filtered down through society as expensive innovations created a demand which justified going into mass production. It is one of the paradoxes of glass as a material that it is made from one of the cheapest natural substances, sand, yet the plant needed to produce it in quantity – float glass for instance – may cost hundreds of thousands of pounds. However, the way glass is being used at the top end of the market today – in banks, rather than palaces – is an indication of the way it may be developed for domestic use in years to come, and therefore worth knowing about.

Photochromic glass, first developed in small quantities for dark glasses, which adjusts according to the light level it is exposed to, is now becoming a feasible proposition for glazing. The self-adjusting property of this glass depends on silver halide crystals in the 'melt' or molten glass mix. Corning, one giant glass manufacturer, have patented a glass called Louverre, which contains photosensitive crystals which block out ultraviolet light. The idea of glass like this is that it screens out the burning glass qualities, while letting light through. It is easy to see how useful this might be in the future for all large glazed areas, such as conservatories, huge picture windows or large rooflights, where the pleasure of being flooded with sunlight has to be offset by the disadvantages of 'cooking' under concentrated ultraviolet rays.

Double glazing is now familiar. Richard Rogers' innovative Lloyds Building, in the City of London, takes the idea a step further with an ingenious

72

RIGHT: *Glass brick windows of varying size fit naturally into the detailing of the Strauss House, Louisiana, which is based on grids of varying scales: tiny for glass bricks, larger for glazing bars, larger still for scored concrete walls. Coloured glass objects on internal shelves light up at night like an impromptu Mondrian.*

ABOVE: *Like many houses in hot climates this one goes easy on windows, but it does feature one twentieth century innovation to do with glass – solar panels built into the sloping roof, which will turn the scorching sunlight to good account.*

system of triple glazing connected to the building's heat exchange system. As sunlight heats up air trapped in the glazed sandwich it is automatically drawn off through the system to be used elsewhere in the building as needed. This is not unlike the way in which solar panels are used to trap and store heat on domestic roofs. It all indicates a welcome flexibility of approach to natural sources of heat and energy.

Mirror glazed buildings, like glass towers but sheathed in reflective but see-through glass, are common in many cities today. In a sense they are a cop-out for a designer, since their purpose is really to disappear, or dissolve in a sea of reflections. But in certain situations, where a new structure abuts or neighbours distinguished old ones, they can make a useful contribution by throwing more light and handsome reflections back, whilst being self effacing themselves.

GLASS PRODUCTION METHODS

Glass is made from one of the cheapest natural substances, silica, or sand, melted and fused at very high temperatures. In physics glass is described as a fluid in suspension and the shattering, when glass breaks and the tension is released, vividly illustrates this.

Roman glass was greenish, thick, shiny on one side but rough on the other, which impaired its transparency. The roughness is thought to have been due to their method of cooling the glass on sand. They made glass by picking up a blob of molten glass on a pipe and blowing through it to make a bubble. The bubble could be spun to make a disc, which would retain the opaque 'bullion' where it had been attached to the pipe, or it could be swung to make a long sausage or cylinder. The cylinder would be slit while hot with a hot iron, then flattened out and cooled, to make a sheet. The glass was cut with iron blades and 'grozed' or nipped them with iron pincers. Thick as old glass was, the wastage must have been considerable. The bulls-eye, or bullion knob so often seen in old windows, was not introduced for its quaintness but because glass was too precious to waste.

Due to the slight variations in texture and thickness, blown glass has a liveliness and surface glitter which is decorative in itself. Anyone owning windows glazed with the original glass should treat

75

them with respect. Missing panes can be replaced with new mouth blown glass, called 'antique' glass in the trade, which have much the same quality. It is a little more expensive than what they are inclined to refer to, a touch contemptuously, as 'agricultural' or float glass.

Most modern clear, or agricultural glass, is made by the 'float' method, whereby molten glass is floated on tin, which also melts, creating a smooth underside almost as clear and shiny as the top surface. The ingredients are 75% silica, plus fluxes, stabilisers, and sodium sulphate to refine the glass and improve its consistency.

Bending glass may not be a technique which we stand in daily need of, but it is interesting to know that many glaziers can bend glass to fit specific situations, from Art Deco lamps to bow windows. Briefly, the glass is laid over an individually shaped mould and gradually heated in an oven till it softens enough to take the shape of the mould.

–ORNAMENTAL GLASS–

In step with the revival of decoration in almost every area of building, there has been a resurgence lately in the making, design and use of decorative glass. There are all sorts of ways in which glass can be worked on to create a decorative effect, enhanced by the translucency of the material.

The oldest, and noblest, use of decorative glass is in glorious stained glass church windows, like the Rose Window in Chartres Cathedral, where light makes jewelled pictures of fragments of coloured glass. The dim religious light cast by stained glass seems generally to have been found unsuitable for secular, domestic buildings, until such full-blooded medievalists as the nineteenth century

William Burges and William Morris introduced it as part of their polychrome interior schemes. Morris and Burne Jones designed some outstanding church windows in stained glass, among the finest of the era, but there are more playful examples of Morris' liking for coloured glass, like the large corridor windows for his Red House, which Philip Webb and Morris hand painted with birds (Webb) and stylised daisies (Morris) in amber and black on plain clear glass.

— COLOURED GLASS —

Glass can be coloured and still remain perfectly transparent. We are so accustomed to thinking of coloured glass in terms of old church windows, in deep jewel shades, or tinted in peachy boudoir on smoky 'celebrity incognito' colours, that it comes as a surprise to find just what a range of subtle, softly coloured glass is available at a good glass merchants. "Hundreds of colours," as one glazier told me. One of the innovations of modern stained glass is to use these gentle colours, like watercolour washes, to filter light softly rather than build up the vivid, jewelled effects of old church glass.

One could easily transform an ordinary glazed front door panel by inserting a delicately coloured patchwork of panes in varying shades. Pale tinted glass blocks very little light – the stronger the colour the more light it blocks – but it colours it noticeably, and looks magnificent against natural light by day, or lit up by electricity at night. Some tinted glass comes in the standard ranges, but these colours are vulgar compared with the more expensive mouth blown, body tinted glass, of which the finest is still made in Britain. To see a good range, look through a trade directory for the sort of

ABOVE: *Decorative glass is undergoing a big revival and the younger artists working with glass are experimenting with all sorts of unusual techniques. This window by Jane McDonald achieves its casual watercolour effect with a mixture of sandblasting, to make it opalescent, and coloured lustres.*

RIGHT: *Richly coloured in the Pre-Raphaelite manner, this splendid window is in fact a patchwork, late Victorian conservatory doors cunningly married with double sash window frames. It graces the Somerset house of Sally and Richard Dennis, dealers in nineteenth and twentieth century ceramics.*

glazier who supplies mainly to the trade and features coloured glass and restoration services. Goddard and Gibbs, in London's East End, for instance, have a large selection of coloured glass available in their own retail outlet, which chiefly services hobbyists interested in making up coloured glass 'roundels' or lampshades in the Tiffany style, put together with copper strips.

Hand Ornamented Glass

There are various types of hand ornamented glass made, usually to a client's brief, by skilled craftsmen/artists. Engraving is done by incising, abrading and scratching the glass with a variety of implements to produce delicate images which show up against the clear glass like frost patterns. There is a revival of this sort of work today, and many artists like Laurence Whistler specialise in it. Most of it is done on commemorative goblets and glass presentation pieces, but a few rich people are commissioning portraits of their houses on panes of glass which are then set into windows – a nice personal touch if you can afford it and your house is worth commemorating.

Engraved glass of the sort which features in old gin palaces is less expensive, but still costly enough to be in demand for restoration purposes. There is some demand for it too for enclosing shower cubicles. Because of its combined frosty/clear nature, engraved glass gives privacy while blocking out very little light. Internal glazed doors sometimes look good with engraved panels.

Simple bevelling and brilliant cutting, which are related techniques, are highly decorative treatments for glass, though they do not give so much privacy. Bevelling involves cutting round the edge of a pane

at a forty-five degree angle. It is most often seen as a finish round mirrors, whose brilliance it greatly enhances, but it can do interesting things to clear panes too. The small bevelled panes in the new Ismaeli centre in London, designed by Sir Hugh Casson, are a good example, subtly jewel-like in the way they refract the light.

Brilliant cutting, a wonderfully evocative name, means cutting faceted and polished patterns into the glass, usually star shaped, or angled, for obvious reasons. These sparkle in the light. In late Victorian times there was a vogue for brilliant cutting flashed glass, that is glass flash-coated with a thin layer of brightly coloured glass. This technique left the faceted incisions sparkling like stars in their coloured surround. Missing panes of decorative glass like this can be replaced by specialist firms.

Painted Glass

'Stained' glass is something of a misnomer, because most windows described as 'stained glass' use a whole range of glass coloured by different means. Only one colour – yellow, from palest straw through to deep topaz, is 'stained', that is clear glass is coloured by painting with a chemical and then fired. Most coloured glass used is body-tinted, that is cut from glass coloured at the raw stage. Where one piece of coloured glass in a window shows more than one colour or outline detail, this will usually have been painted. Professionals use metal oxide colours mixed with a little glass flux, or enamels, all of which are fired to make them permanent, like glazes on pottery. Variations in tone are often arrived at by finely hatching through the dried paint, before firing, to reveal the clear glass

ABOVE: *Another interesting way to block out an ugly view. In this case an idyllic pastoral scene has been sand blasted on to clear glass which has then been set in front of a panel of blue glass.*

RIGHT: *To create privacy as well as reinforce the strong black and white scheme of this small bathroom, the window panes have been painted with a black lattice pattern. Painting simple designs on glass is not difficult.*

beneath, rather like shading with a pencil only in reverse.

The problem for amateurs with painting glass is to make it at all durable. Special transparent glass paints can be obtained which look effective, but firing is needed to fix colours through years of cleaning and weathering. However, if permanency is not your aim and you would like to turn a dull window into a feast of translucent pattern, glass paints are fun to experiment with. The colours may need building up gradually, with several successive layers, as they are very pale otherwise.

An alternative, and very simple method of altering and screening a problem window is to spray white or coloured car paint over the glass through a tightly stretched panel of cheap cotton lace, the sort that turns up as a cast off in flea markets. This will not last for years, but it gives something of the effect of Victorian engraved glass at a fraction of the cost.

TYPES OF DOMESTIC GLASS

Because the majority of homes have clear plain glass in their windows many people are unaware of the wide range of glass that can be used for glazing. Some effects are purely decorative while others incorporate special properties which make them particularly suitable in certain situations.

ORDINARY DOMESTIC GLASS
Ordinary glass, sometimes called plate glass or annealed glass, is invariably of the 'float' type. It comes in various thicknesses for different types of window frame and different uses and is widely stocked, inexpensive when compared with other types and easily cut to size. Its main disadvantage is that it breaks into long lethal shards.

REINFORCED OR SAFETY GLASS
Toughened glass is up to five times as strong as ordinary glass. The toughening process is achieved by subjecting the glass to heat almost to melting point and cooling it quickly by blowing air on to both surfaces simultaneously. The cooling process locks the outer surfaces of the glass in a state of high compression and the central core in compensating tension. Once toughened, the glass cannot be cut or subjected to further processing so it must be cut to size before treatment and any alterations

81

LEFT: *By slotting slatted shutters into a curving wall of glass bricks this bathroom combines maximum natural lighting, and ventilation, without loss of privacy. The sleek look of glass bricks perfectly suits the functional style of the room.*

such as a hole for an exterior fan or bevelling must be done beforehand. Most types and thicknesses of glass can be toughened.

Toughened glass looks the same as ordinary glass except in strong sunlight when spots or blotches may be visible from certain angles. It is not part of the standard stock of retailers as each piece has to be cut to size before it is toughened, so it must be ordered specially. It stands up well to impact by blunt objects but if the outer skin is punctured by something sharp the glass breaks into thousands of very small particles with dulled edges that don't injure. It is enforced for use in possible danger areas, such as glazed doors or French windows; anywhere, in fact, that glazed areas are likely to collide with small children. Other factors which might indicate the use of safety glass are where glazing has to withstand high winds, snow or hail. Fire resistance and even, alas, bullet proofing are other safety aspects which glass manufacturers are being asked to look at.

LAMINATED GLASS

Laminated glass consists of a tough flexible interlayer of plastic membrane called polyvinyl butyral (pvb) sandwiched between two panes of ordinary glass. It can be made with as many layers as necessary, right up to the point where it is bullet proof. Laminated glass will crack if struck but the broken glass continues to adhere to the pvb so is unlikely to injure and still acts as a barrier.

Laminated glass can be incorporated into double glazing units and is also quite effective in reducing noise because of the damping effect of the interlayer. It blocks sunlight and so helps protect fabrics from fading and by using a coloured interlayer can create a tinted effect.

WIRED GLASS

Wired glass is ordinary glass into which a fine wire mesh is incorporated. This impedes visibility to some extent and it is not particularly attractive when used in windows. Its main advantage is that it acts as a barrier against flames and smoke in case of fire. It is in constant use in rooflights and overhead glazing where breakage might cause damage or injuries to objects or people below, and is also proof against leaping cats, extremes of weather and burglars.

When wired glass breaks, the wires hold the glass together. Take care when handling broken wired glass as in addition to the danger from glass the wires themselves may protrude. Wired glass can be cut to size as required and is generally held in stock by glass merchants.

SOLAR CONTROL GLASS

This comes in different types, with the effect achieved by tinting or coating. Solar control cuts down solar heat gain through windows and reduces reflected glare. The tint or coating does marginally reduce the amount of light coming through the window, but the eye can adjust to this relatively quickly. This type of glass often has a reflective outer surface which increases privacy in the home because people cannot see through it. When used in a double glazing unit, with the inside of one of the pieces of glass coated with low emissivity coating, energy costs are reduced and warmth

82

ABOVE: *A detail of the celebrated all-glass bathroom Paul Nash designed for dancer Tilly Losch in the thirties. Nash was inspired by the unexplored potential of glass, its extraordinary colours – like the deep midnight blue seen here – its subtle textures and reflectiveness.*

inside the home increases in winter, while during the summer heat from the sun is kept out.

OPAQUE GLASS

There are scores of types of patterned glass available, ranging from the simple milky opacity of ground glass to the more complicated types of traditional or modern patterned design. These are created by passing molten glass between textured rollers. This type of glass can be toughened if necessary and some can also be tinted.

Patterned glass is useful in areas like bathrooms or lavatories where privacy is required. The designs tend to be undistinguished, but if you want to block an ugly view or simply stop people looking in, they are the most economical solution. One way to escape the public lavatory effect of this sort of glass might be to use it more creatively, mixing effects with some ground panes plus some patterned ones, like a lace edged handkerchief.

DOUBLE GLAZING

Double glazing can be a mixed blessing. It offers a number of advantages of an unaesthetic type but, if care is not taken, can spoil the look of your windows. You have only to look down any suburban street to see that an ordinary but pleasing and well proportioned building can be made to look unattractive and out of scale by the indiscriminate ripping out of the original windows and their replacement by a standard fitting manufactured with no design in mind.

On the plus side, double glazing acts by sandwiching a layer of still air between two surfaces. It can cut fuel bills significantly in some homes but even so is unlikely to pay for itself as quickly as other types of insulation. It does increase comfort in the home and can make areas like bay and bow windows and inside patio doors usable areas rather than no-go ones in cold weather. It can also to

83

ABOVE: *Different designs of patterned glass can add to the appeal of a window or be used to screen out an unattractive view or provide privacy within a room. There are hundreds of designs available, ranging from plain reeding to elegantly ornate.*

some degree reduce condensation. Because the inner pane is not as cold as a single pane would be there is a less immediate change of temperature, which means less moisture forms. However, many people have been persuaded to part with hard earned cash for double glazing and have found that their condensation problems do not go away. It is important to have adequate ventilation in the room and there is, alas, no easy cure for many cases of condensation.

Double glazing can in some circumstances help to cut down on noise; triple glazing is even more effective in this area. Some window frames and walls are simply not strong enough to take the weight of triple-glazed glass and you should obtain professional advice from an architect or structural engineer before attempting to instal it.

Double glazing comes in two forms: sealed units and coupled frames. Sealed units consist of two panes of glass which are hermetically sealed together by a factory process, trapping a layer of air between them. They can be fitted into existing window frames if they are a suitable size and shape but are usually sold as replacement windows and fitted into new frames.

Coupled frames consist of two separately glazed frames which are hinged at one side so that they can be opened separately for cleaning. Secondary sashes are designed to fit over existing windows on the inside. They offer the advantage that they can be taken down in summer and stored, thus allowing you to open the original windows; something that is difficult, if not impossible, when secondary sashes are in place.

DO-IT-YOURSELF DOUBLE GLAZING
There are several alternatives ranging from the annual to the permanent type. For a long-term job you can buy kits consisting of flexible plastic channelling, rigid plastic or aluminium. You cut them to size and single glaze them to fit over your existing windows. You can buy various types to fit sash or casement windows. If installed correctly these kits do a good job, but the finished effect tends always to be a bit Heath Robinson when viewed from the inside.

A less permanent solution is to buy a special touch-and-close blind kit. A piece of thin but rigid plastic sheeting cut to size is fitted with Velcro to the the window frames. This can be rolled up on the

same principle as a blind, but unless it is obscured by curtains, you will have to live with the sight of the fixing whenever you do so. If not installed very tightly this type of double glazing tends to make a slight rustling sound and might obscure the view through the window.

Even more ephemeral is the special type of plastic film which you cut to the size of the window and press round the surround. You play a hair dryer over it until it is as taut as a drum skin and leave it in position for the cold months. This type does not rustle but does create visibility problems.

FRAMING UP
If you are choosing professionally installed double glazing involving replacement windows it is important to think carefully about the materials from which they are made. From an aesthetic point of view it is almost always preferable to replace with the same material and window design that the original builder used. However modern materials such as aluminium, stainless steel and upvc can be successfully used to replace wood frames in certain situations; it is usually the replacement of a group of small, often interestingly designed panes of glass with a large flat expanse that gives a house a 'dead' look from the outside. Double-glazed wooden replacement windows tend to be more expensive than other types partly because each frame has to be custom built.

FINANCING REPLACEMENT DOUBLE GLAZING
Double glazing by replacing windows is one of the more expensive home improvements and you may need to extend your mortgage or borrow money to do it. It is very important to use a firm with a good reputation; preferably one which has been around for some time. Get two or three quotations for the work and be sure to check the terms offered very carefully in terms of the materials used and the guarantee. Find out if the installers will remove your old windows or whether you will have to dispose of them yourself. Ask how long the work will take from start to finish and whether the installers will make good any damage to existing interior or exterior decorations. Inspect the selection of window furniture carefully and, if necessary, be prepared to pay more for a design of your choice rather than accept something you do not like or which does not fit in with your decor.

Because double glazing is a high capital venture, many firms have gone bankrupt along the way. It is therefore worth employing a firm which is a member of the Glass and Glazing Federation who operate a special insurance scheme whereby if one of their members goes bust they guarantee to arrange for another to complete the job. It won't save you any money but could ensure that you are not left windowless with no prospect of the replacements ever arriving.

——— GLAZING A WINDOW ———

Reglazing a window is a fairly simple DIY job and a skill that is well worth mastering. Glaziers may be hard to come by in your area and it can be cold, not to mention a security risk, to leave a window covered only with cardboard or plastic sheeting. Do not, however, start by reglazing a large picture window; go for something small and simple.

Begin by removing all the broken glass from the window. Wear tough gloves such as gardening gloves and goggles to protect your eyes from flying shards. If you are working on a window directly above a pavement or garden area either put up a warning sign or cordon off the area while you work. With a small hammer tap out the pieces of glass, starting at the top of the window. Wrap the broken glass in old newspaper and either take it to a local authority tip or place it in a cardboard box, seal it and mark it clearly 'broken glass' for the benefit of the refuse collectors.

Next, chip out all the old putty from the rebates (the angled grooves in which the glass fits). With wooden frames, remove all the headless nails (called sprigs or brads) which hold the glass in place; with metal frames collect the metal clips used for this purpose as they can be used again. Treat the window frame for rot or rust according to the instructions on page 67. Apply wood primer to any bare areas of wood and also inside all the rebates to prevent the oil from the putty being absorbed into the frame.

Measure up for the new glass. Most windows are glazed with 3mm or 4mm glass but plate glass for picture windows is usually 6mm. Double glazed sealed units vary in thickness but this can be checked from the width of the rebate. Measure the height and width of the window frame and subtract 3mm from each measurement – which should be taken from inside the rebates. Check the diagonals to ensure that the window is square or rectangular. If it is uneven you will need to take a series of measurements to allow for this. While you can cut glass to size yourself, a mistake could wipe out any saving over paying a glazier. It is probably quicker and easier to let an expert do the job.

Buy a universal putty mixture for fixing the glass into position on both wood and metal frames. Using a pointed scraper or trowel, place a strip of putty along all the rebates. Put the pane of glass into position and press firmly all round the edges to squeeze out as much putty as possible. Take care not to press in the centre of the glass or you will break it.

On a wooden frame use small headless nails (sprigs or brads) to hold the glass in position. On a metal frame use the metal clips you have saved. If necessary, appply more putty to cover them and give a good finish all round the pane. With a putty knife, smooth it off evenly. With the straight side of the knife point work firmly across each edge of the frame to press the putty against the glass. As when icing a cake, moistening the knife with water from time to time will help it run smoothly. Take care that the outside edge of the window is finished at an angle along the bottom which will let rainwater run off easily. With the point of the knife remove any surplus putty. It should be allowed to dry for at least a week before repainting.

——— CLEANING WINDOWS ———

Clean windows regularly, especially if you live in an urban or traffic-ridden area. Otherwise the panes of glass will become dingy, let in less light and fail to sparkle when the sun shines on them. Clean both sides of the glass at the same time so that you see the full benefit of cleaning and do it on a day when there is little sunshine as this causes the windows to dry too quickly and look smeared.

You can use a proprietary cleaner in liquid or aerosol form or a cheaper home-made product. Aerosol cleaners are easier to use in fiddly areas such as round leaded lights and can get into corners which are difficult to reach with a cloth or brush. If you choose the home-made variety, use tepid water with a little washing up liquid or methylated spirit; the latter is good in cold weather as it stops the water from freezing on the glass.

85

Windows, or at least apertures in walls, may have been around for thousands of years, but curtains, drapes and blinds are comparatively recent. Before glass began to be used in the sixteenth and seventeenth centuries, windows were small, set high in walls for ventilation as well as light and were closed off against bad weather or intruders by wooden shutters. Glazing made larger windows practicable, but glazed windows were such a luxury, and the light flooding through them so welcome, that it would have seemed perverse to cover them up again.

The windows which Vermeer used in so many of his paintings are uncurtained. In fact, hangings over doorways seem to have preceded hangings over windows. Where walls were hung with cloth – tapestry for the rich; sturdy, woollen cloth for the bourgeoisie – a length would be nailed over the door, to be looped back when it was inconvenient. It may well have been these door hangings which inspired someone to extend the idea over windows, keeping in more warmth and masking the dark expanse of windows at night. Once a good idea has occurred, it is surprising how speedily it can develop and reach great sophistication. By the end of the eighteenth century, to judge from contemporary prints and paintings, all reasonably prosperous windows, at least in reception rooms, would have been curtained or hung with blinds, or both, and in many cases they had wooden shutters too, for security and warmth.

Soft furnishings were originally taken care of by upholsterers, an art which reached its zenith in the mid-nineteenth century. Contemporary pattern books show windows caparisoned with a lavishness and inventive detailing never equalled before or since. In their zeal for upholstering, the Victorians often carried a window treatment not just across the windows but also across the spaces between. The first 'soft wall' had been invented. Cosiness, the 'snug', became a domestic ideal throughout Europe in the first half of the nineteenth century. Some delightful examples of cosiness gone coquettish were the tented, entirely fabric-hung boudoirs for elegant ladies to read novels, play the piano, drink tea or receive their friends in, and in these the windows were invariably treated en suite with the walls – an inspired ruse for making any room look luxuriously cocooned, and one still much copied today.

By the beginning of this century a fierce reaction had set in. The young found the heavy, fusty drapes of earlier generations stultifying. Hygiene was an important new shibboleth and early household manuals stress the importance of letting in light, air and sunshine. The first windows designed to do this, the horizontally expanded metal framed windows so characteristic of modern housing, must often have found themselves curtained (to their designers' secret despair) in the gaily flowered cretonne, just touching the sill, which the manuals tended to favour. Metal frames and flowered cretonne must still have been relatively advanced; if windows had a uniform, it remained what it still is, the decent veil of lace, muslin, or latterly polyester, which is such a conspicuous feature of dark northern industrial streets, prim suburbs and today's legacy of less tower blocks.

Architects continue to bemoan the absurdity of ruffled sheers dolling up their nice clean lines and blocking out the light, air and view they have been at such pains to provide. But this only proves that

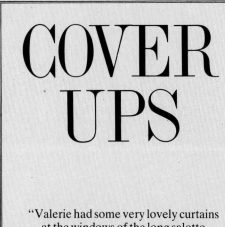

COVER UPS

"Valerie had some very lovely curtains at the windows of the long salotto looking on the river, curtains of queer, ancient material that looked like finely knitted silk, most beautifully faded down from vermilion and orange and gold and black to a sheer soft glow."

Things
D. H. Lawrence

LEFT: *All done, and how masterfully, with stripes. Schinkel's fabric-hung room in the Schloss Charlottenburg is one of the masterpieces of the genre, perfectly simple yet thoughtfully detailed (note the bed canopies) and irresistibly chic, with its demure looped back curtains and coordinated chair covers.*

householders, in the main, value privacy and decency above other considerations. 'Home' is an inward-looking concept today, focussed upon that other magical window, the TV screen.

──── FURNISHING FASHIONS ────

Fashions move more slowly in interior decoration than clothes, but window dressing these days is almost as eclectic as people dressing. The fabric blind, roller, pleated or festoon, is undoubtedly the ongoing success story of recent years, ousting sheers as the new uniform in window dressing. There are cogent reasons for this – fabric blinds use comparatively little fabric, most of them are a straightforward DIY proposition, they allow the degree of light to be adjusted and they suit most styles of window, including many problematic ones such as tiny dormers and narrow hall windows where conventional curtains would be out of place.

Another type of blind which is in for a big revival is the slatted plastic Venetian blind. In good colours and smart finishes they have come a long way upmarket from the grubby white plastic which gave them a bad image in the sixties. Today they are popular with the trendy young, who have adopted one of the chic retro looks between Art Deco and razzle dazzle Memphis. Blinds like these remain the best solution for the horizontally elongated windows, often metal framed, which were such a feature of houses and flats built in the last fifty years. Red and shiny, sleek grey for a toned down thirties style room or, most dazzling, in a chromed finish which glitters by lamplight.

ABOVE: *The simplest of blinds are often the most effective. Here, Roman pleated but in a magnificently moody midnight blue, they shed a mysterious light over the dramatic pictures and furnishings in a room which has 'designer' stamped all over it.*

RIGHT: *These simple frames, painted the same deep blue as the walls, and filled in the centre panel with shirred cotton print, produce an attractive variation on the window shutter. The light is filtered and privacy obtained without taking up too much space.*

ABOVE: *Tall, round-headed windows like this trio look distinguished but are a problem when it comes to cover-ups. Blinds look fussy, conventional curtains too voluminous. In this case the ideal solution is severely classical drapes, in a colour matching the wall, gathered to an arched heading and simply looped back on each side.*

Their clean cut effect suits the sleek, sparse rooms with geometric rugs and tailored covers that belong to this latest version of urban style.

A contrasting look which is also increasing in popularity is what America calls succinctly 'country', and it is just as popular in cities as in genuine rustic dwellings. People with suitable windows plunder old picture books, postcards from Greece, photographs of Provencal houses and so on for the sort of simple, nostalgic window treatments which add a lot of atmosphere for very little cost. Simply painted surrounds, sturdy painted shutters or a casually hung scrap of scrunchy cotton lace are all part of this style.

At the top end of the market, where cash is not the first consideration, we seem to be in the midst of a revival of full dress curtaining as lavish and opulently detailed as anything dreamed up by the Victorians. Cascades of fabric, lined and inter-lined for draping ability as well as warmth, flow from intricate pelmets which are swathed, swagged, fringed and tasselled. Curtaining like this can never be cheap because of the sheer yardage involved, but it adds romantic softness and complements a currently fashionable interior style which might be called elegant dishevelment.

—————— **ARCHITECTURE** ——————

The period style, height, size and positioning of windows all play a part in deciding on a window treatment. Tall, slender period windows of the early and late Georgian type, with deep reveals and shutters, clearly demand a quite different approach from small cottage windows or wide shallow metal framed ones. It is always a good idea to do a little research into period treatments and a look at old prints, picture books or a history of interior decorating can help solve problems such as whether to hang curtains inside or on top of the window frame, whether blinds can coexist with shutters and so on. Often, a typical treatment of the period can still be the most attractive. For instance, the tall, narrow, deep set windows in early eighteenth century houses should never be smothered in lavish curtaining and pelmets, which obscure their elegant lines and block out too much light. The period treatment was either to leave them uncurtained and use the shutters at night, or to hang festoon blinds at the head of the windows, or to hang narrow but heavy curtains either side from a plain pole.

Light is often the main consideration when dealing with old cottage windows, or indeed any windows in buildings with thick walls. Anything too dressed up, like festoon blinds, jibes with their sturdy geometry. The traditional solution was to stand a big geranium on the windowsill. Another would be to hang a square of old tatting or Nottingham lace, which can be looped back on sunny days. For larger, but still rustic-looking windows, slatted shutters painted to fit in with the room scheme look handsome and traditional. These work best with casement windows which can be opened fully to let in air and sun. The point to remember is that where the view outside is the attraction, and the window merely serves as a frame, the less elaborate the window treatment the better.

Horizontally-expanded metal framed windows are difficult to curtain, but can be seen at their best with a clean cut, hard edged treatment such as plain fabric or Venetian blinds which accentuate

91

ABOVE: *Shutters do not have to be slatted to admit light. When they are decoratively pierced, the cut out shapes make a bold pattern against the light. Designs such as these are relatively simple to cut from plywood with a jig saw.*

and make a virtue of their period lines. Attempts to soften them with pelmets or sheers look out of place. If you really crave a softer look, the best solution would be a combination of fabric blind and wall to wall curtaining in some neutral but elegant fabric which makes a fabric wall at night. In the daytime the curtains can be drawn right back while the blind, in the same fabric, bridges the space and frames the window.

Probably the hardest window of all to cover up elegantly is the classic suburban bay window with its two narrow sash windows set obliquely either side of the main front window. Hanging curtains in groups, a pair each side of the central window and one each side of the outer windows, blocks out most of the light. The solution which seems to work best is to have all the curtains for the whole window expanse drawn back either side of the bay, with a good looking pelmet treatment running round to give a visual connection and fabric roller blinds to diffuse the light if necessary.

CLIMATE

Climate is a decisive factor in window dressing. Those pierced screens which the fierce North African sun punctures so glamorously look forbidding, even prison like, against cold northern light. The heavy voluminous drapes which make for cosiness on cold winter nights are oppressively fusty in breathlessly hot climates where one's whole instinct is to let in as much air – though maybe not light – as possible. Normally, the hotter the climate the less clutter one wants around a window, which is probably why the traditional solution of slatted shutters, which let the air through but filter hot sunlight, is still one of the best. Alternatively, nothing looks cooler than long curtains in some light translucent fabric such as lawn, muslin or calico fluttering in the breeze from a ceiling fan. There is a wonderful shot at the beginning of Visconti's *The Leopard* where all the windows of a Sicilian palace, stunned in noonday heat, are suddenly aflutter, and the inside temperature almost palpably drops.

Unexpectedly, this same idea of framing windows in light translucent material – not the same thing as covering them with sheers – is an old tradition in one of the coldest European countries, Sweden. The fact that Swedish homes are well

warmed and properly insulated makes flimsy curtaining possible, but the explanation for their preference is probably a wish to let in all the light and sunlight possible in a country where so much of the winter is spent in near darkness. With a traditional Swedish style in interior decorating currently coming up strongly on both sides of the Atlantic, the gentle coloured serene look known as Gustavian, this artless form of curtaining now crops up in fashionable interiors everywhere. In rooms which are otherwise busy and colourful, the simplicity of slender falls of plain white or creamy fabric with a matching swag looped over the curtain pole looks refreshing and attractive.

This sort of careless style has to be done with conviction though. I have seen two versions of this look, one in a very elegant Paris flat where the casual window draperies nicely offset the formality of grand antiques and carefully worked out colours; the other in a tiny flat decorated on a shoestring, where the same cheap but gutsy cotton sheeting was used both to create swags and folds around the windows and to cover every piece of furniture in the room. The overall creaminess had class, and a few prints and cushions in sizzling colours prevented the room from looking like the night before the country house sale.

CHOOSING A STYLE

When deciding on a suitable and attractive window treatment, the only point to think seriously about in the current eclectic mood is probably appropriateness. It is a usefully vague word, taking in all aspects of suitability from the fatness of your purse to the annual mean temperature, the existing architecture or lack of it and the spread of colours, objects and fabrics which will make up the style of your rooms.

Getting the window dressing right makes such a dramatic improvement to a room that it is sensible to sort through the options before committing yourself. Unless privacy is urgent (and you can always pin up sheets in the meantime if it is) it is always best to leave the windows to last. Get the main colour areas in a room sorted out, which are also as a rule the most expensive, and the window treatment should then follow as a matter of course. By then, too, you will know your room better: how much sunlight it gets, whether you want to invite

ABOVE: *The Victorian bay window, that trickiest proposition to deal
with, decoratively speaking, gets the full cover-up treatment here.
Cascades of curtaining, looped back each side, plus swagged pelmet
and pendant drapes, combine with plain blinds to smother the
problem, and soften any awkwardness.*

the view in or block it out, what your colour scheme needs in the way of softening or contrast, whether you enjoy your windows plain and unadorned or cannot wait to camouflage them with masses of fabric, or whether you want the ultimate two-decker window cover-up (blind plus curtains and pelmet) which can disguise the original shape of the window aperture completely.

——— CHEAP AND CHEERFUL ———

Cheap cover-ups can be very stylish. Old textiles can still be found at bargain basement prices on market stalls or in junk shops and with a bit of imagination can be converted into blinds or simple curtains which give their patterns and workmanship their due. Making one's own blinds is a perfectly feasible proposition with so many kits on the market. Alternatively, cheap ready-made roller blinds can be ordered in a variety of standard sizes, in plain materials like holland, and can then be stencilled or painted freehand with special fabric paints to fit in with a room's decorating scheme.

Lace, festooned or draped over windows, is becoming something of a romantic cliché, but it still has a lot of mileage in it for an unashamedly feminine look in bedrooms and some Victorian front rooms. The lace curtains of one's grandmother's generation are still being sold off cheaply. Bleached, mended, starched and used generously rather than stretched, they are still one of the most glamorous solutions around.

For an original and inexpensive look, hand painted curtains are becoming popular again, for the first time since the Omega workshop made a splash with them in the twenties and thirties. Young designers now paint on lightweight canvas or cotton sheeting in big bold designs and soft chalky colours. This is an idea one could adapt quite easily, maybe just painting wide stripes in delicious ice cream colours.

Making curtains is a slow business when properly done, but not too difficult for anyone with some dressmaking experience. The problem is often the sheer cost of fabric. The grandest curtains, made by top decorating firms, use twice as much fabric as the conventional formula of two and a half times the window width and this lavishness undoubtedly contributes to their effect, but you can get away with skimpier curtains if you pad

95

LEFT: *The curtains here are as uncomplicated as tent flaps, but because they are made of the same rich red that covers the walls and sofas in this striking room, the whole effect is one of sumptuous simplicity. Note the patterned roman blinds which pick up colours in the stencilled frieze.*

and quilt them, possibly around some of the pattern motifs. Rather than skimp on an expensive fabric, it looks better to be generous with a cheap one. I have seen the cheapest unbleached calico used very stylishly, handled as if it were silk, for voluminous trailing curtains, bordered in a contrasting colour and topped by a very deep, gathered and shaped pelmet flounce.

— Deciding between Curtains and Blinds —

While cost may be a deciding factor when you come to choose between curtains and blinds (blinds use less fabric and usually work out much cheaper) what you should really consider is the different effects that can be produced in both categories. This book shows a wealth of imaginative ideas for treating windows but in some rooms certain problems may prevent you doing what you would really like.

Radiators are often sited under windows, since this is a position in which they are particularly effective. Your choice is either to have short curtains which do not cover the radiator or to hang long ones and allow your expensive heating to go, literally, out of the window. If you have set your heart on floor length curtains at a particular window, then your only solution would be to move the radiator, but this is a major upheaval in a room which you are not doing up from scratch.

Window seats produce the same problems as radiators but can be taken out. However, windows with window seats often overlook spectacular or pleasant views and it might be better to retain the pleasure of having them to sit on and to fit the window with a decorative blind or two which would have

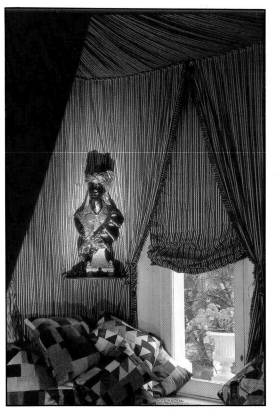

the advantage of not being crushed in the way that curtains might be when people lean against them.

Shelves or large pieces of furniture sited right next to a window frame can make it difficult to pull back curtains. Here too blinds might be better.

The following pages deal with the types of fabric needed for making curtains and blinds and give instructions on how to achieve different effects.

——— Choosing Fabric for Curtains ———

Choose curtain fabric to suit both your windows and your budget. Large windows definitely need fabric of the right weight to hang well but with small windows you can sometimes get away with a dressmaking fabric. It's important to note that furnishing fabrics are specifically designed to be durable in use, hang well and resist fading, abrasion and attacks from moth or mildew. Dressmaking fabrics are designed to be easy and comfortable to wear and often come in patterns which are not suitable when exposed over the larger-than-dress-size area of a window. Upholstery fabrics are different again; they are usually too thick for making up into curtains and may not drape well. Those which contain a proportion of linen will crease when hung. Many curtain fabric manufacturers make matching upholstery fabrics in a different weight for those who want to produce a total matching effect.

When shopping for curtain fabric, take samples of other items in the room such as carpet, any existing upholstery fabrics and wallpaper or a piece of paper with the paint shade on it. Ideally, ask if you can have a good-sized sample to take home to look at in

96

ABOVE: *Cut off from the outside world, this seating alcove tented in cheap striped cotton, with Roman blinds and curtains to match, makes a dashing foil to blackamoor busts and a heap of bright cushions.*

RIGHT: *Doing it all out in nicely textured neutrals is a great way of handling a small room like this study. Creamy curtains frame a bamboo blind kept lowered to let light in but keep the view out.*

the room itself. Some stores make a charge for this, others require a deposit which is refundable when you return the swatch. Look at the fabric in both natural and artificial light as these will give different effects.

Think about your budget. Do not buy some fabric, intending to return for the rest when you have more money, or you may find that the second lot does not match exactly.

Consider cleaning carefully. If the curtains are intended for an area such as a kitchen or bathroom where they will get dirty quickly, choose a fabric which will wash well. Curtains intended for living rooms and bedrooms will not need cleaning frequently unless you live in an industrial area, so you can choose a fabric which needs to be dry cleaned.

Ask the sales assistant to hold the fabric vertically, draped into a couple of pleats. It is impossible to tell what curtains will look like when staring at a horizontal piece of material rolled off a bolt.

You may be able to calculate the amount of fabric needed yourself, but it is a good idea to have this measurement checked in the store. Take a sketch of the window and its dimensions with you plus the heading tape, or be prepared to tell them what heading tape you will be using.

Check the length of fabric thoroughly for flaws as it is being measured and ask the the assistant to double check it for you. Manufacturers usually mark flaws by stitching coloured thread into the selvedge, but there may be other flaws which have not been picked up.

Bear in mind that large patterns require more material in order to match up the drops or pattern repeats. Stripes and small or random patterns are more economical in this respect. You must allow for an additional pattern repeat for each drop of fabric you are buying.

If you are planning to wash the curtains when they are made up you should wash the fabric twice before sewing it, using the temperature recommended for the fibres. If you are using pre-shrunk fabric just tack the hems and do not stitch them down until the curtains have been washed for the first time as slight shrinkage may occur.

——— Types of Fabric ———

A glossary of all the fabrics that could be used for making curtains successfully would take a complete book. There are so many mixtures of fibres, both natural and synthetic, often with specialist brand names, that it is difficult to be specific. The following is a selection of the most widely used and available types.

Calico is a firmly woven cotton fabric with a matt finish. It is usually used for lining soft furnishings and garments but is an excellent curtain fabric because of its weave and is, for those on a budget, an excellent value buy. It is usually available in a limited range of colours but can be dyed to virtually any shade required.

Canvas is also cotton, tightly woven in a plain or rib weave but may be linen or man-made fibre also. It is very strong and relatively cheap. It does not drape very well so it is not suitable for pleated curtains but makes excellent blinds and can also be used for the tab type of café curtains.

Chintz is a type of closely-woven cotton which is given a glazed finish by the application of chemicals. It is stiff to work with but hangs beautifully and makes excellent curtains. The glaze helps the fabric to resist dirt but is gradually removed with cleaning and unfortunately re-glazing is a service that is virtually impossible to find.

Cotton can be used either on its own or in combination with other natural and synthetic fibres. It is a strong fibre, usually woven closely into a firm fabric which takes dye and printing well and can also be given a number of special treatments to render it shrink resistant, flameproof, water repellant and crease resistant.

Cotton sateen is usually used for curtain lining and comes in a good range of colours. However, it makes good inexpensive curtains if a sufficient fullness of fabric is used.

Denim is firmly woven and can be used to make attractive curtains, especially if given some form of appliquéd finish. It should be washed before making up to remove any dressing and cope with any shrinkage.

Dupion or antique satin is made mainly from synthetic fibres with a slub weave along the warp which gives it a similar appearance to raw silk. Its drawback is that it frays immediately when cut so needs care when sewing; you should allow for this when measuring up.

Felt is an ideal material if you want to make curtains quickly as it can be cut to size without the need for side seams or hems. It makes excellent

99

LEFT: *Today's curtain couture, which costs a fortune unless you make it yourself. Yards of glazed chintz are edged with a piped contrasting pleated frill and looped back with tasselled tie backs dyed to match. The curtains are topped by a lavish valance shaped in a gently graduated curve.*

café curtains as it is easy to cut the required shapes along the top evenly.

Gingham is a useful fabric if you are not lining curtains since the pattern shows through on the wrong side. Buy curtain rather than dressmaking weight as the latter is very light and produces poor draping and a billowy effect.

Lace is an open fabric made from cotton or man-made fibres. It comes in a variety of weights and designs with some tradi-tional patterns having names such as Chantilly or guipure. Some lace has ribbon woven into it for a further decorative effect. Lace makes up into excellent, very pretty curtains which can, depending on the weight of fabric and density of pattern, be used either as nets or as the main curtains them-selves. If you are lucky enough to find old lace bedspreads or curtains in a brick-a-brac shop or auction they often sell cheaply because they are dirty but are easily washed and can be used for curtains or blinds.

Lawn is really a dress weight fabric made of tightly woven cotton, linen or man-made fibre. It comes in very attrac-tive designs and is good for small curtains but lacks the body to be suitable for long full-length drapes.

Mattress ticking is a good buy for the budget con-scious, with the added bonus that no pattern matching is needed and there is no wastage when cutting the drops. Be sure to wash it first to remove any dressing and allow for shrinkage.

Sheeting is another good choice for anyone on a budget. Cotton and polyester/cotton sheeting can be used for curtain making and small curtains can also be made out of old worn sheets which are still good in parts. Patterned sheeting is useful if you want to match your curtains to your bed linen and

there is not an appropriate curtain fabric available. *Silk*, because of the way it is produced, is very expensive indeed and does tend to be affected by sunlight, although strong in other respects. Many man-made fibres are combined to make fabrics which look similar to silk but are easier to care for. If you must have the real thing, be prepared to pay heavily for it.

Tweed may be made from natural or synthetic fibres in a variety of colours and weaves. Loosely-woven weaves need care in making up as they tend to stretch. Lock the interlining and lining at more frequent intervals than specified on page 111 in order to keep the fabric in shape.

Velvet is made from natural and synthetic fibres in a variety of pile densities and woven on to different backings. It can be difficult fabric to work with as the right sides tend to slip easily when placed together. Velvet should always be tacked before machine sewing; if slipperiness is a bad problem, put tissue paper between the two pieces of fabric and pull it out after machine stitch-ing is complete. Velvet is usually hung with the pile running down the curtain to prevent it catching dust and spoiling its appearance. Take great care, especially with plain velvets, to ensure that each drop runs in the same direction.

Curtain Lining Fabrics

Lining curtains and some blinds improves their appearance and the way the fabric hangs. Linings look more attractive than the wrong side of curtain face fabric when viewed from outside the window and make turnings and hems look neater. Linings also protect the main fabric from fading, dirt and

ABOVE: *Windows look better for not being overdressed in hot climates. A flutter of light, diaphanous fabric at the window looks refreshing. Even better, as on this little curtain, when the fabric is embroidered with a strong design that shows up against the light.*

condensation and some lining fabrics have special properties which increase insulation and/or keep out light.

Where a lining is sewn into the main fabric, the curtains or blind will need to be dry cleaned to ensure that the two different fabrics do not shrink at different rates and cause puckering. Where curtains need frequent cleaning, you may prefer to wash the face fabric, in which case a detachable lining is a good solution (see page 112). Detachable linings can be washed separately from the main fabric if necessary. If any shrinkage occurs this can be accommodated by adjusting the heading tape on the lining, since there is no need for the lining to be gathered to the same degree of fullness as the face fabric.

Cotton sateen is the most commonly used lining fabric. It is relatively lightweight and firmly, though slightly unevenly, woven. Never tear it or pull a thread to get a straight line for cutting; use a T-square or set square and ruler. Cotton sateen comes in a good variety of colours; it can be used imaginatively to give a hint of colour through a paler face fabric or to provide a toning or contrasting effect where a lining shows at the edge of a curtain or the base of a pelmet or valance.

Thermal linings provide the same advantages as cotton sateen and also help to reflect heat back into a room in winter and keep heat out of a room in summer. They are also useful for eliminating draughts around badly-fitting windows. Note that their thermal properties only apply when the curtains are drawn across the window. One type, a flocked cotton or polyester/cotton mixture, is coated with a dense compound of acrylic and can be washed. Another, milium lining, is made by coating cotton sateen with a solution of aluminium particles which produce a silvery effect on one side of the fabric. Milium should be used with the silver side facing the back of the face fabric and must always be dry cleaned.

Blackout linings provide standard and insulation benefits and are also impermeable to light. They are a good choice in bedrooms, especially for young children who tend to wake up at first light and for people who work shifts and find it difficult to sleep if a room is light. Blackout lining is thicker than the other types but drapes well and does not spoil the hang of a face fabric. When making up blackout lining you need to be sure that your machine needle is sharp and to adjust the tension to accommodate the extra thickness.

CURTAIN INTERLINING FABRICS

Interlining curtains adds body to thin and medium weight fabrics and improves their draping properties. It is not necessary with thick, densely woven fabrics nor if you are using thermal or blackout lining, since it duplicates many of their properties. Interlining cuts down on outside noise (useful if you live near a busy road or on a flight path), helps to insulate a room by trapping air between the layers and reduces the amount of light entering a room. Interlining is used as a sandwich between the face fabric of a curtain and its lining. Details of how to make interlined curtains are on page 107. Interlined curtains should always be dry cleaned.

Bump is the most commonly used fabric and is made of coarsely-woven brushed cotton. Once cut, raw edges should be hemmed or overlocked.

Domette is also made of brushed cotton but is less blanket-like than bump and feels more like flannelette. Cut raw edges should be hemmed or overlocked. Synthetic raised interlining is made of a mixture of fibres stitched and bonded together and is thinner and lighter than bump and domette.

Note that interlining curtains increases their weight significantly so make sure that the curtain track you are using is strong enough and sufficiently firmly fixed to take them.

THRIFT TIP
If you are trying to do up a home on a budget you will be on the look out for bargains all the time. Don't neglect windows in favour of furniture. Make a note of all your window sizes and keep them with you together with the actual amount of fabric you'll need (this will depend on the heading tape/type of blind). Sales, especially the closing-down kind, market stalls and some antique or bric-a-brac shops can be good sources of bargain fabric, but you must be sure that you know how much to buy since it's unlikely you'll be able to match it up in the future.

CURTAIN HEADING TAPES

Hand-made curtain headings take more time and trouble than the commercial variety but do allow 101 you to create exactly the effect you want and to tailor the size and distance apart of any pleats to the size of your window. They are made from buckram, available from curtain specialists and department stores with extensive fabric sections. Virtually any of the effects described and shown below can be produced by hand using either buckram or soft tape. Page 111 tells you how to create French pleats. For more specialist effects, such as smocking, you should consult a handbook devoted solely to curtain making and, if possible, attend a class in order to gain practical experience before tackling a major pair of curtains, especially if you are using expensive fabric.

Decide what effect you want from your curtain heading before selecting a fabric. Your choice of heading will depend to some degree on the weight and weave of fabric and the track you intend to use (see page 105) as well as how much money is available. Some types of heading use considerably more fabric than others. Many retail outlets have small sample curtains on show which give an idea of how a heading looks when pulled up. If not, ask a sales assistant to pleat up a small section for you to give you some idea of the finished effect.

As a general rule, it is worth noting that a plain or small patterned fabric can take a more elaborate and highly pleated heading than one with a large pattern where you want the motif to be visible when the curtains are pulled across the window.

There are basically two types of commercial heading tape. With one you get fitted cords which pull up into the type of pleat required plus hook pockets into which you fix the appropriate hooks. The other type comes with a continuous row of hook pockets and you use the hooks themselves – single, double or triple – to create the type of pleat you want, at the distance apart which suits the width of the window.

TYPES OF CURTAIN HEADING
Standard gathered tape is the cheapest available and comes in both cotton and synthetic fibres and also in a range of colours. It creates a fairly sparse type of gather so is most suitable for short curtains made from lightweight fabrics where the heading will be hidden under a pelmet or valance. It is not suitable for long curtains in heavier fabrics such as velvet, even if a pelmet is to be used, as the pleating will hardly show.
Pencil pleats use a lot of fabric, up to two and a half times the width of the window if you want tight, even pleats and up to three times the width for net curtains. The depth of the pleat varies from 4-15 cm (1½-6 in), which gather up to a maximum of about 36 pleats per metre/yard with certain brands. It is also possible to buy a spaced pencil pleat tape; this requires the same amount of fabric but produces a softer drape and allows pattern to be seen more clearly. Because pencil pleating is

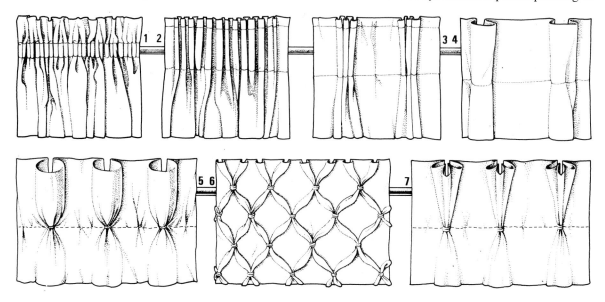

ABOVE: *Different forms of curtain heading. (1) Standard gathered (2) Pencil pleats (3) Triple pleats (4) Cartridge pleats (5) Goblet pleats (6) Smocked heading (7) Triple doubled French pleats.*

102

ABOVE: *In a style which might be described as MGM Regency, bouffant curtains of shimmering silk are caught up so they hang in puffy tiers against a mild background of sheer curtaining, hiding an undistinguished window in a London dining room.*

very tight in its effect it does not pull back as far as other headings so you need to allow plenty of room for the return (the technical term for the space taken up by pulled back curtains) and should extend the track beyond the edges of the window if you do not want to shut out light.

French, or *pinch*, *pleats* may be single, double or triple according to the type of hooks used. The depth of pleat ranges from 4-13.5cm (1½-5½in) and two to two and a half times the width of the track is required in fabric. This type of heading is stiff to work with since it is designed so that the flat stretches between the pleats stay upright rather than sagging forward. If you are using ready corded tape you will get an even effect more easily by choosing a brand with three rather than two tapes which support the height better. If you are making pleats using special hooks, you can decide for yourself where to place pleats and where to have space between.

Cartridge pleats are produced from a commercial tape which can also be used to give a goblet effect. Cartridge pleats, unlike French pleats, are the same width both top and bottom, giving an almost box pleated effect. This is a good heading tape to use on heavy fabrics where you also plan to have a pelmet or valance. To turn the cartridge effect into goblets, hand pinch the base of each pleat and stitch so that it stays put. To keep the open goblet effect, stuff a little tissue paper or cotton wool into the pleat.

Specialist pleats can be used to create unusual effects with curtain headings but are best used on plain or lightly patterned fabrics where their effect can be seen to full advantage. Examples of specialist pleats include smocking, trellis and Tudor ruff effects and it is also possible to buy heading tape which gathers up into flat box pleats.

Lining tape is used when you are making curtains with detachable linings (see page 112). It is usually made of cotton and comes in colours to match the range of standard coloured lining fabrics available. You may need to pay slightly more for a brand which does not show when you are looking through the outside of the windows.

USING COMMERCIAL HEADING TAPES

When you have worked out what length of tape you need, allow for a little extra so that you have scope to decide where the pleats come. Most commercial tapes are sold with instructions for sewing them on and gathering; ask for these when you buy.

However expert you are at sewing, always tack curtain heading into position before machine stitching. The tapes have a certain amount of stretch woven into them and tend to shift out of position unless anchored firmly. Always sew both sides of tape in the same direction. Go one way along the top, finish firmly and then start again at the original end when sewing the bottom. This prevents the tape shifting and the pocket for the hooks becoming unaligned.

Choose the correct sewing thread (natural or synthetic depending on the fibres of the face fabric) and either match it to the main colour of the fabric or select a tone darker. Adjust the tension of the machine by stitching a small sample of fabric and heading tape together.

When you have secured the ends of the stitching, pull up the curtain heading, working evenly. Knot the ends of the cords, anchor them around a table leg or door handle and gently work the heading tape until gathered to your satisfaction and adjusted to the correct width. Do not cut off surplus cord but wind it round a cord tidy or cleat. You will need to be able to let out the pleating when the curtains are washed or cleaned.

TRACKS FOR HANGING CURTAINS

There are several points to consider when deciding what type of track, pole or rod you want to suspend your curtains from. Some tracks are designed to be visible, even when the curtains are drawn across the window, and should be regarded as an integral part of their decorative effect. Other tracks are designed to be as inconspicuous as possible and to blend in almost invisibly with the window surround when the curtains are drawn back.

Not all curtains can be hung on all types of track as weight is a critical factor. Most track manufacturers have specifications for what weight of curtains can be hung along particular lengths of different types of track and you should take account of these when choosing. If you are buying a track to hang some curtains which are already made you should weigh the curtains in advance so you can tell the sales assistant both the track length required and the weight of curtains to be hung on them. If the curtains are not yet made up weigh the fabric together with any lining and interlining. Put curtains or fabric in a large plastic bin liner and weigh them on bathroom or launderette scales.

As a rough guide, the following weights can be supported on tracks measuring up to 3.6m (12ft):

Lighweight duty (usually plastic)   6.81kg (15lb)
Medium weight duty (usually plastic)   9kg (20lb)
Medium to heavyweight duty
     (usually plastic or metal)   13.6kg (30lb)
Heavyweight duty
     (usually top-fixing metal)   36.3kg (80lb)

However, it is essential to check the manufacturer's specification before buying as these weights do not apply to all brands in these categories.

QUALITY CHOICE
Curtain tracking is one of those areas where you get what you pay for. Cheap tracks are usually less stylish than more expensive ones and also tend to be of inferior quality and liable to bend, with gliders which do not run smoothly and require frequent applications of lubricator.

Cheap track is fine if you are on a tight budget, doing up rented short-stay accommodation or just fitting a lightweight curtain over a small window somewhere like a lavatory or utility room. But if you have spent money on quality fabric and made up attractive curtains it is a false economy to buy cheap track.

INSTALLATION
Straightforward curtain track is fairly simple for a competent do-it-yourself handyman to install, but where long lengths are involved or you are fixing track around a multi-angled bow or bay window, it may be better to have the job done professionally. Specialist curtain stores normally employ qualified track installers, who will ensure that the track is fixed securely and may also be prepared to dress the curtains for you. Unless you are very expert it

105

ABOVE: *Stencil artist Lyn le Grice has made a place of medieval simplicity of her bedroom in an old Cornish millhouse. The gravity of linenfold panelling, used as a bedhead, is echoed by the nun's wimple shape of the simplest muslin curtains caught up to their pole either side of a small window.*

is sensible to employ a professional to fix track with complicated electrically controlled cording.

MEASURING UP

Track does not have to start and finish at the sides of the window frame. If you do fit this length, especially at narrow windows, you will find that the curtains (particularly if they are thick and/or full) will cover part of the glass when drawn back and not only exclude light but possibly spoil the shape of the window. Where space permits allow the track to extend past the edges of the window frame so that when drawn back the leading edge of the curtain is just over the edge of the frame.

If the track is very long you will need to have extra fixings to prevent it sagging when the curtains are drawn. Remember that the fixings at each end of the track must be particularly strong and secure since these will be supporting the entire weight of the curtains when they are drawn back. You may not have any choice about where to place fixings but it is worth noting that top fixings which go into the ceiling or top of a window embrasure can take a lot more weight than the side-fixed type which fit on to a wall or frame face.

If you have a concrete lintel over your window you may find it difficult to drill satisfactorily to take track fixings. If so, it may be better to fit a strong piece of wood along the lintel and fix the track to this. This is also a useful solution in older properties where the walls and plasterwork are crumbling or in poor condition.

TYPES OF TRACK

Brass poles may be solid brass or steel plated with brass. To avoid brass tarnishing and the consequent cleaning which could make curtains dirty, choose brass poles which have been lacquered. Before buying, look not just at the pole itself but at the fixings and finials (end pieces). These are sometimes made of plastic painted with a brass colour and can look cheap and nasty.

Metal tracks are very strong and a good choice for heavy curtains. However, they tend to look functional rather than decorative. They are a good choice for bow and bay windows as they can be bent round the curve thus allowing you to make up curtains which treat the window as a whole. Lightweight duty metal tracks are easily bent but the heavier ones need to be bent and fitted by professional installers.

Plastic track comes in different grades and although lightweight in itself can be used for heavy curtains provided the correct type is chosen. Some plastic tracks are designed to bend but these are usually fairly lightweight and not suitable for heavy curtains which require the support of a metal track. Some plastic tracks are designed so that you can paint them or cover them in wallpaper or fabric to go with the room's decoration. Check this carefully when you buy as you can only cover tracks which are designed so that the runners can move freely afterwards.

Wooden poles come in a variety of finishes which allow you to choose the one which best goes with

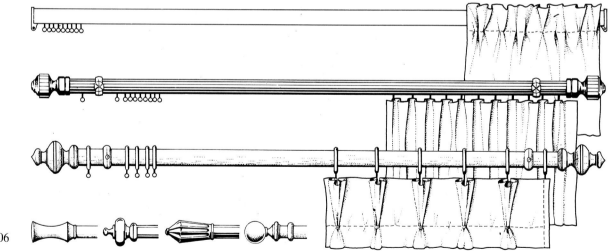

ABOVE: *(from top to bottom) Simple plastic track, metal pole, wooden pole, a selection of finials.*

your window frame, furniture or general colour scheme. Because wood has a tendency to warp, it is important to select the correct diameter of pole for the weight of the curtains. Wood is probably not a suitable choice in rooms or conservatories where the atmosphere is very hot. Untreated wooden poles allow you to create your own finish by staining, varnishing or painting in the shade you want. If you are painting a wooden pole it is best to use a matt finish product as gloss scratches easily and may also create reflections.

Wood-effect poles may be made of metal or plastic with a grained finish. Plastic 'wood' poles are lighter than the real thing so may be more suitable in certain circumstances. Steel based 'wood' poles are very strong and will not warp or sag in the way that real wood may.

RINGS AND RUNNERS

Rings and runners are designed to go with specific tracks so it is essential to buy the correct ones. They may be sold with the track or pole as a kit or bought separately. If the latter, take advice on how many you need for the width of the curtain as if they are not sufficiently well supported they will hang unevenly. When buying, you should also work out whether you need finials, overlap arms (to allow one leading edge of the curtains to be drawn over the other to ensure there is no gap between), cording sets or draw rods.

You will also need the hooks to link the curtain heading and track. Be sure that these are compatible, depending on whether you are organising curtains or track first. Some curtain headings require particular types of hook which are not suitable for suspending from certain types of ring or runner. Take a sample of either hook or runner when going shopping.

CORDING SETS

Using a cording set makes pulling curtains easier, particularly if they are very long and heavy. It also protects the fabric from soiling and, in the case of pile fabrics like velvet, from showing hand prints.

Some curtain tracks come ready-corded while with others you fit the cording yourself. Although it is fairly easy to fit a cording set to a simple run of track, it is best either to buy ready-corded or to get a professional to cord up long or curved runs of track. If you have two or three curtains of the same width it is possible to draw them simultaneously using just one cording system.

Electric cording sets remove the effort of pulling a cord but work only on straight runs of track. They are operated from a control box which should be sited somewhere convenient and must be installed by a professional. Some brands can be operated by a remote control in a similar way to a television set. One advantage of electric cording sets is that they can be programmed with the use of a time switch so that they will draw automatically at a preset time of day; useful if you wish to conserve heating or to give the impression that the house is occupied when you are away.

DRAW RODS

Draw rods are a less complex method of drawing curtains without touching the fabric. They are sold in pairs and each one is attached to the leading runner or hook of each curtain. Once the drawing action in either direction is completed the rod will hang behind the curtain.

——— MAKING INTERLINED CURTAINS ———

The method of curtain making described here is for French or triple pleats using a hand-made heading of buckram and interlining and lining the curtains. This effect is one commonly used by professional interior designers, but the method itself can also be followed if you are making curtains using one of the commercial heading tapes described on page 102. Follow it up to the point where the heading is fixed and then follow the instructions given by the tape manufacturer. If you are using a different heading tape to French pleating check the recommended fabric width.

Instructions for making unlined curtains and separate linings are given on page 112.

107

ABOVE: *Draw rods enable you to move curtains without marking the fabric with your hands. They also make drawing heavy curtains easier.*

MEASURING UP

Measuring up is of vital importance with curtain fabric since even a slight misjudgement can cause a bad pattern match or curtains which are fractionally too short and spoil the appearance of the room. Before cutting the first length you should decide what measurement you want the finished curtains to be and, with patterned fabric, where on the curtains you want the pattern to be seen to best advantage. If, for example, you have a large motif you will probably want it to appear in its entirety in the middle of the curtains even if it is truncated at top and bottom.

As a general guide, curtains should be either floor or window sill length since anything in between tends to look as if you did not have or could not afford enough fabric. However there are obviously exceptions to all rules and unusually shaped rooms or windows may require special treatment in terms of curtain length.

Floor length curtains should finish about half an inch from the floor itself if they are to draw easily without catching. If you are measuring for curtains in a room which is not yet carpeted be sure to allow for the height of any floorcovering and underlay when calculating the length of the curtains. Some people prefer their floor length curtains to trail on the ground but bear in mind that these can present hazards in homes with elderly peope, small children or pets. To achieve this luxurious flowing effect they need to be made of a soft fabric that drapes well rather than a heavy more rigid one, and the folds on the floor will need careful weighting and arranging if they are to continue to look good.

Sill length curtains should finish just short of the sill so that they draw easily and do not pick up dust and possible condensation from it. At the top of the curtain the measurement should be taken according to the type of track you are using and whereabouts on it the hooks are fixed.

When you have established the final overall length, add an extra 25 cm (10 in) to allow for hem and heading and also take into account the extra drop needed for pattern matching. Calculate the width according to the type of heading being used (see page 102) and the width of the fabric you are using. Where appropriate you can use a half width on the outer edge of each curtain to obtain the right amount of gathering.

PREPARATION

When making curtains it is essential to work on a large flat surface. Although it is possible to do it on the floor, a carpet or other soft finish may effect accurate pattern matching and will undoubtedly give you backache. If possible use a large dining table, preferably covered with a piece of chipboard so that you do not score or mark the surface, or hire a couple of trestles from your local hire outlet. If you are planning to make a lot of curtains it is probably worth investing in a pair of trestle legs and large piece of chipboard which can be dismantled and stored easily when not in use.

Although there is a lot of hand sewing in curtain making you will need a machine for joining lengths of fabric, sewing on heading tape and making pleats. If buying a new machine, choose a free arm model that is large and strong enough to cope with thick fabrics and which does zigzag as well as straight stitching. Make sure you understand and have practised the various machine stitches before letting it loose on large expanses of fabric.

An iron is essential for pressing the work as you go along. Use the correct setting for pressing whatever fabric you are working with and take care with a spray and steam facility that you do not watermark delicate fabrics. If you want to iron large expanses of fabric it may be easier to lay a blanket over your worktable rather than use an ironing board. You may need to use an extension lead to allow your iron to reach a good distance from the socket outlet.

For accurate measuring you will need a tape measure that does not stretch, a T-square or set square for making accurate right angles and tailor's chalk for marking your measurements on the fabric.

For cutting out you need a large sharp pair of scissors; bent-handled ones are more comfortable for cutting long runs and lefthanders will do best with specially designed scissors.

Pins and needles should be sharp and rust-free or they can mark the fabric. Buy the sharpest you can and throw away any that become blunt or crooked. Do not leave pins in fabric any longer than necessary. A tip for the clumsy: if you prick your finger and get a blood spot on the fabric this can be removed by rolling up a piece of white thread, moistening it with your spit and gently rubbing until the mark disappears.

Use the right thread for the type of fabric: cotton with natural fibres and synthetic thread with synthetic ones. As a general rule match the colour of the thread to the main background colour of the fabric, aiming for a slightly darker tone.

To ensure patterns are matched exactly you need to hold fabric steady. A set of weights and clamps make this easy. Weights can be those from kitchen scales or bricks covered with wadding to prevent them damaging the fabric. Clamps can be bought from stationers, do-it-yourself shops and picture framing outlets.

CURTAIN JARGON EXPLAINED

Three terms used extensively in curtain-making instructions need to be clearly understood. The *face fabric* is the main curtain fabric, the one which faces into the room and to which the interlining and lining are attached. The *leading edge* of a curtain is the one by which it is drawn, in the centre of the window. The other edge of the curtain is referred to as the *window edge*.

CUTTING THE LENGTHS

Before cutting the first length check right along the fabric for any flaws which might spoil the appearance of the finished curtain. Ideally this should also have been done in the store, but not all flaws show up under artificial light so take a good look at the fabric in natural daylight. If you find serious flaws you may wish to exchange the piece for a complete perfect length. If you have knowingly bought substandard fabric try to ensure that the flaws are cut out or made into the window rather than the leading edge of the curtain.

Lay the fabric right side up on your flat surface and mark off the first length with tailor's chalk. Check the length again and then cut, using a T-square, set square or book to give you a right angle. Never tear fabric as this pulls the threads and may distort the piece.

With tailor's chalk, mark an arrow on the wrong side of the piece to indicate the top of the curtain and the way the fabric should be hung. With some patterns it is difficult to establish which way up they should hang and with plain fabrics hanging lengths which are not all cut off the roll in the same direction can mean that they do not look matched up when the light catches them.

Heat your iron to the appropriate temperature for the fabric and iron the seam allowance under. Now match up the pattern against the next length to be cut, making sure it fits exactly along the fold of the seam allowance you have ironed. Use weights and clamps or heavy books to hold the two pieces of fabric in position while you do this. Do not pin at this stage since pin marks are visible on many fabrics and can damage some, such as chintz.

Cut each length in this way, ironing the seam allowance and matching the pattern exactly. If there is any waste between the lengths because of pattern repeats cut it off at this stage so that no cutting or matching errors can occur; a stepped effect will result if you don't do this.

JOINING UP

Join one width at a time rather than tacking or pinning them all before machining. Using the pressed edges and the weights and clamps match up the pattern exactly, then slip stitch tightly through the crease all along the seam. Open up and use the stitching as tacking and the pressing line as a seam guide. Alternatively pin, taking care not to pin through the top fabric where it will mark, open up and stitch along the line. Trim the top and bottom if necessary after matching each seam so that you do not make a wrong pattern match when adding the next length. Measure each length after joining to ensure it is correct.

As you join the various lengths work across the window from one side to the other rather than making up one curtain from left to right and the other from right to left. Any half widths which are being used should be positioned at the window rather than the leading edge.

Iron open all the seams on the wrong side, using the tip of the iron and placing a piece of fabric *below* the seam allowance to prevent marks showing on the right side.

FIXING THE INTERLINING

Allow plenty of time for fixing the interlining to the face fabric since when it is done the pair of them should be treated as one piece of material. If you do not concentrate while doing it you can end up with the face fabric puckered or the interlining not fixed firmly enough so that it billows and creates a messy looking curtain.

Cut the interlining to the same size as the main curtain fabric. Join the lengths by overlapping the

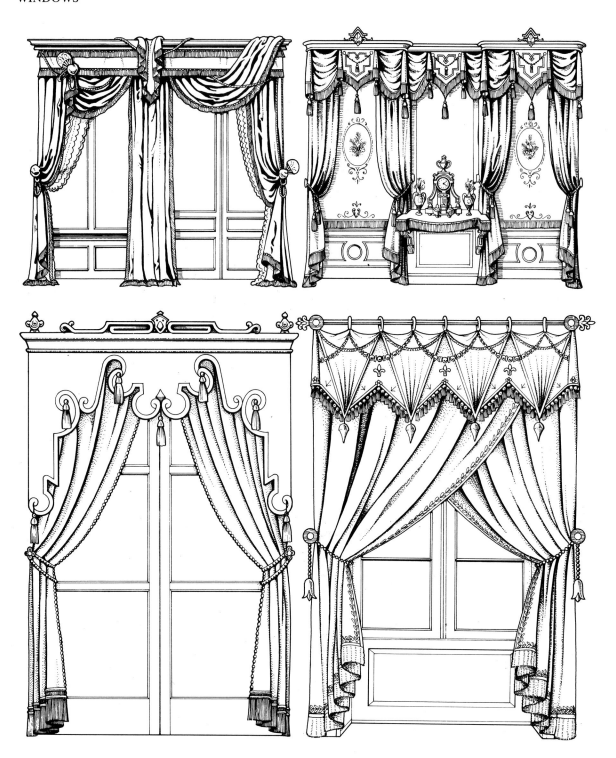

ABOVE: *Different ways to drape a window, as suggested in a nineteenth century pattern book. For those who like this opulent approach to cover-ups, swags, tails and pelmets with a seemingly endless variety of decorative trimmings and tie-backs, can all be used to add interest to a plain window or enhance a decorative one.*

edges by about 2.5cm (1in) and machine stitch down the centre of the overlap using a small zigzag stitch. Trim off the surplus on each side.

Lay the interlining over the face fabric (keeping the furry side inwards if you are using bump) and match up the seams on the main fabric and interlining. Smooth until it lies flat.

Working from the leading edge and using a locking stitch, fix the interlining to the face fabric with a loose stitch, picking up just a couple of threads from the face fabric with each one. Run a row of stitches from top to bottom at 30cm (12in) intervals on large curtains, less on smaller ones. Leave about 20cm (8in) free at the top and bottom to allow for the heading and the hem. Lock more firmly along the leading and window edges.

MAKING THE HEM

Many professionals advocate leaving curtains unhemmed until they have been hung for some time to allow the fabric to drop but you could end up with a crooked curtain if you do not square off the bottom. There is also the risk with large curtains that you never get round to hemming them at all, because the effort of removing them from the track, hemming and then re-dressing is too much.

You have cut enough fabric to make a 15cm (6in) hem, which is long enough for you to let it down if cleaning causes shrinkage.

On the first curtain, turn up a hem of 7.5cm (3in) and press. Turn up another 7.5cm (3in). Press again and then unfold the hem and mitre the corners. To do this, fold in the corner of the fabric until it makes a diagonal line across the point where the pressed lines of the side seam and main hem line cross. Press this diagonal and fold up the hem into position again. You may need to cut off some of the surplus fabric if it is very thick to prevent a bulky appearance at the corners. Insert a 2.5cm (1in) circular weight into each corner and stitch into position. If you are using it, this is the stage at which to lay weighed tape along the hem line. Stitch the hem into place catching the top edge of the mitre to the interlining but not through the main fabric.

With the second and any subsequent curtains, lay each alongside the first and match the pattern along the hem line. Turn up 15cm (6in) and press, then turn in the 7.5cm (3in) fold and stitch the hem.

HEADING UP

When the hem is complete, measure off the finished length of the curtain and press a fold along the top. Do not worry if the pattern is not straight here as this will be disguised when the fabric is gathered. It is much more important to have a straight hem.

Cut a piece of 15cm (6in) fusible buckram long enough to go right across the width of the curtain and lay it inside the top fold at right angles to the leading edge. Tack it into position, making sure the tacking goes right through the main fabric; any needle marks will be hidden when the gathers are made.

MAKING THE LINING

Cut the lining fabric to the size of the main curtain and join the lengths together. Lay it over the interlining and match up the seams. Turn in so that it lies 2.5cm (1in) from the edge of the leading edge and 2.5cm (1in) from the top. Fold in along the bottom edge so that the fold runs across the points of the two mitres. Run rows of locking stitches vertically so that the lining is fastened to the interlining in the way the interlining is fixed to the face fabric. Slip stitch up the leading edge and along the top and then stitch the other fabric edge. From now on treat the three layers of fabric as one piece.

PLACING THE PLEATS

At this point you must decide how large you want your triple pleats to be and how far apart. Curtains look best if the first pleat is not so near the edge that it makes drawing a problem. Ideally you should leave half the space between the pleats at the leading edge of each curtain but this is not always possible. Remember that if your curtains are to be hung on an overlapping track you should allow for this when siting the pleats. Do not have gaps of more than 17.5cm (7in) between pleats or it will look as if you have skimped on the fabric. Always keep the same gap between pleats. Mark the position of each end of each pleat with a pin.

At this stage you must decide whether to trim off some of the interlining or leave it in position. With some fabrics the four layers of material make a rather bulky heading; with others all four are needed to give rigidity.

Using double thread, tack down the length of each pleat from the top of the curtain to 2.5cm

(1 in) below the bottom of the buckram. Machine down each pleat three times, always stitching in the same direction and with each row of stitching on top of the one below. Remove the tacking thread. With your hands work each pleat gently until it forms a loose tube. Press each tube into a triple pleat, making sure the pleating is even. Either stab stitch into position at the base of the pleat, using a strong buttonhole thread, or stitch across the front of the pleat with matching thread making sure you create a firm hold.

The triple row of stitching down the pleat makes a strong base into which the pin hook can be fixed so that the curtain can be hung. If the curtains drop a lot or become shortened by cleaning you can adjust their height by moving the position of the pin hook.

——— Making Lined Curtains ———

Lined curtains are made in the same way as inter-lined ones and are less bulky to handle unless you use one of the special thermal linings (see page 101) which also add bulk. When locking lining directly to the face fabric take care not to let the stitches show through.

——— Making Unlined Curtains ———

Unlined curtains are useful in situations where fabric needs to be washed frequently (kitchens and bathrooms) and where the light-excluding and insulation properties of lining are not necessary.

To make an unlined curtain, cut and join the lengths of fabric as described on page 109. Use a flat fell seam to join the pieces to prevent light showing through the stitches once the seam is pressed. But bear in mind that this does produce a row of stitches which show on the right side so take care to use a thread which will show as little as possible. Machine stitch down the seam line and press open. Cut one of the seam allowances back to 6 mm (¼ in) and fold the other raw edge over it. Stitch down. Hem and head the curtain as planned.

——— Separate Curtain Linings ———

Curtains with separate linings tend to look less tailored and more fussy than those with sewn-in linings but are useful if you may need to wash them frequently or when you have summer and winter face fabrics but do not want the expense of two sets of linings.

Detachable curtain linings are made with their own heading tape (lining tape) and hang on the same hooks as the main curtain. Ideally they should be stitched at intervals along the leading and window edges to hold lining and face fabric in position and to prevent them flapping in draughts. For separate linings you need less fabric than for the main curtain. One and a half to two times the width is usually plenty.

——— Coping with Errors ———

It is, alas, only too easy to make mistakes when making up curtains, either by failing to concentrate or because you are inexperienced. The main problem is usually with the cutting of the fabric so that you end up with a mismatch which means your curtains will not be the length you intended. It is of course possible to rush out and buy extra material but you may not be able to afford this, may not be able to obtain your original bargain or may not be able to get an exact colour match.

If you cannot retrieve your error in these ways you will need to think again. Obviously long curtains can be turned into short curtains but this is not always the solution. To keep the original length it may be necessary to even up the cut pieces by inserting a sewn-in border of different fabric – perhaps a patterned one with plain curtains which could be echoed in a matching pelmet or, with patterned curtains, a plain inserted strip. Do not just add a different fabric to the bottom of the curtains or it will be obvious that something went wrong. Remove at least 15 cm (6 in) from the bottom of the curtains – more if they are long ones – and insert the extra strip at the most appropriate point. Try to pick up the added fabric at some place in the decor of the room so that it looks as if you meant to incorporate it in the first place.

——— Dressing Curtains ———

If you set curtains into the folds in which you want them to fall and leave them in position for about a week, they will be fixed into the fabric and will always drape in the same way when the curtains

ABOVE: *Luxurious moiré fabric, used on walls and for curtains,
lushly gathered and frilled, makes a subdued foil for the icy glitter of a
Venetian style mirror and console in mirror glass.*

are pulled back. Tightly gathered headings like deep pleats will pull back into shape automatically, but widely spaced gathers such as French, cartridge or goblet pleats need to have the spaces between the pleats arranged in the way you want them to fall permanently.

As a general rule, when hanging widely-spaced pleats from a track you should adjust the spaces between them so that they fall forward when the pleats are drawn back. When hung from a pole these pleats look best if the spaces between them are pushed back. But at this stage you can adjust the hanging until it produces the effect you want. Once you have achieved this, leave the curtains in the drawn back position and tie pieces of tape or ribbon round them, working down from top to bottom and tying at roughly 30 cm (12 in) intervals. Do not tie so tightly that horizontal creases form

on the fabric, nor so loosely that the shape is not held. Leave the curtains tied, ideally for a week but for not less than three days before undoing the tapes and putting the curtains into use.

CURTAIN TIE-BACKS

Tying back curtains can allow more light into a room, prevent very full curtains looking enormous when in the drawn back position and also create interesting decorative effects in the way in which they hold the curtains in position.

The most pedestrian type of tie-back is a metal holding device designed to keep the curtain in position when pulled back. These hold-backs range from the plain to the ornate and are made in metals ranging from alloy to solid brass. They are fixed to the side of the window frame or the wall and the curtain bulk pushed into them.

Shaped and stiffened tie-backs can be designed to enhance the curtains' effect and may be made of matching or contrasting fabric. They are made in the same way as pelmets, using pelmet or ordinary buckram; the size will depend on the weight of curtain they have to support. Tie-backs are usually fixed to a small cleat positioned in the window frame or on the wall.

Softer tie-backs can be made by stitching thin tubes of fabric, stuffing them with wadding and plaiting them together. Cut the strips of fabric twice as long as you want the tie-back to be and allow 1.5 cm (⅝ in) seam allowance. Stitch along the length at one end and turn inside out. You may need to use something like a blunt bamboo cane to help with this if the tube is quite thin. Use the cane again to help stuff wadding evenly through the tube and do not fill it too full or the plaited effect will look overstuffed. Turn in the other end and slip stitch. Stitch three tubes together and plait. The plait can either be finished by stitching the tubes together at the other end or by tying thin cord round a few centimetres from each end.

Cords and tassels are also used for tying back curtains and you can make your own or buy them ready-made. Attractive effects can be achieved by twisting or plaiting several lengths of different coloured cord, perhaps picking out different colours in the curtain fabric. There is a wide range of colours available and specialist curtain shops can usually track down any particularly subtle

ABOVE: *A selection of tie-back designs showing how you can decide at which point you want to loop back the curtains, either to create a special effect or to allow more or less light to enter through the window.*

shade which is required. Other types of tie-back can be made from ribbons, braid, lace and other trimmings.

PELMETS AND VALANCES

Pelmets and valances are used to create a decorative effect at the top of a curtain or blind. They can be used to disguise an ugly track or window top, to allow you to economise by using standard curtain heading tape or to alter the shape of a window and make it appear larger (by fixing the heading outside its perimeter) or smaller (by fixing it inside).

When choosing the design for a pelmet it is important to keep it in proportion to the height of the room and the size of the window. As a rough guide it should be either one sixth of the total finished length of the curtains or blind or as a ratio,

allow about 3.75 cm (1½ in) of pelmet for every 30 cm (12 in) of drop. Simple pelmets can easily be made at home but more complex shapes or very long runs are best left to professional curtain makers unless you are convinced that you can create an even design and do the arithmetic required for it.

Wooden pelmets can be bought ready-made in a variety of wood finishes and colours such as white, ivory and gold. Intricate wooden pelmets were a standard fixture in many nineteenth and early twentieth century houses and can sometimes be found in antique and junk shops and in Britain in architectural salvage outlets. This type of pelmet is designed to be seen as part of a room's integral decor but basic pelmet 'shelves' are made of materials such as chipboard and designed to have a stiffened fabric pelmet attached to them. The

ABOVE: *One of the most imaginative examples of style on a shoe-string in recent years. This delightful Suffolk sitting room makes brilliant use of paint, on the floor as well as walls, but the master stroke is plain curtains, given a period elegance by a contrast border and pelmet, piped and edged with braid.*

pelmet board is fixed with brackets like a shelf and fabric covered buckram attached to it either with small tacks or with touch and close fastening.

A buckram pelmet may be a straight box-like affair, cut into curved or geometrical shapes or trimmed with tassels, bobbles or ruching. Usually the curtain fabric is used, but this is not essential and the pelmet can be designed to pick up other furnishings in the room, to be plain above patterned curtains or vice versa. The important issue is to get the proportion of pelmet to curtain or blind correct so that it does not dominate the window to the detriment of the curtains. It must look right both when the curtains are drawn across the window and when they are drawn back.

You can buy special pelmet buckram which is stencilled with a selection of designs so that you can cut the one of your choice evenly. Otherwise you should use buckram and make a card template of your chosen design. Before marking it on to the buckram, measure the full length of the pelmet and make sure that the design is centred at the correct point. Decide whether you want each end to finish in a complete section of the design if it is, for example, scallops, or whether you would prefer to finish with half scallops. Cut your template accordingly; you can adjust the design as necessary.

When you have cut the buckram prepare a long strip of interlining fabric cut about 5 cm (2 in) deeper than the buckram. Place the buckram on top of the interlining and trim or nick the interlining where necessary so that you can fold it over the buckram all the way round. If you are using special pelmet buckram this is impregnated with glue and you just need to damp it round the edges

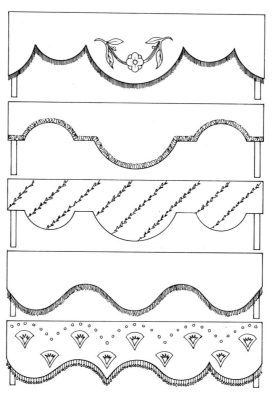

and press the interlining on to the dampened areas using a warm iron. If you are using ordinary buckram you will need to use a flexible adhesive to fix it in place.

Make up the face fabric, joining pieces as necessary and pressing the seams open. It should be cut about 5 cm (2 in) larger than the interlining so that it too can be stuck down over the edge of the interlining, using the same method. But first tack it into position so that the fabric does not slip and any pattern remains correct in its horizontal position. If you are using a fabric which frays easily, overcast the edges before fixing it to the buckram. When it is stuck down slip stitch the corners so that they lie flat.

Trimmings of any kind should be applied to the pelmet after the face fabric is in position but before it is lined. Pelmets need to be lined on the wrong side or the wrong side will look unattractive from outside the window and may also be visible when people inside are standing near the window.

Cut the lining fabric to the size of the pelmet allowing 2.5 cm (1 in) turning all the way round. Place it over the wrong side of the pelmet, turn in the allowance and pin into position, taking care that at no point does the lining obtrude over the edge of the pelmet. Slip stitch into position.

To put the pelmet into position either sew a strip of touch and close fastening along the back top edge and glue the other strip along the pelmet board or stitch a piece of cotton tape along the back, making sure that it is firmly fixed through the buckram but that the stitches do not show on the right side. Stitch right along the bottom edge and then along the top edge, leaving a 2.5 cm (1 in) gap every 10 cm (4 in). Fix the pelmet on to its board by

ABOVE: *Pelmets can be cut to the exact design required and decorated or trimmed to suit the style of the window and the style of dressing, be it curtains or a blind. The more ornate the outline of a pelmet, the less need to add extra trimmings.*

inserting a strong drawing pin into each gap and pressing it firmly into the board.

MAKING A VALANCE

A valance is, in effect, a short curtain which is sited at the top of a window over curtains or a blind. Unlike a pelmet, a valance is soft, falling in gathers or pleats unstiffened by buckram. It can be hung either from a pelmet board, attached by drawing pins or touch and close fastening, or by a valance rail which may be separate from or part of the main curtain track.

To make a valance you can use either buckram to make your own pleats (see page 111) or a commercial heading tape. Depending on the type of heading used you can calculate the width of fabric needed. Because a valance covers the top of curtains these can be made with standard gathered or other inexpensive heading tape if you need to save money since the gathering will not be seen and cheaper headings require less face fabric. The depth of a valance is worked out as for a pelmet unless you are aiming for a particular effect. Allow 7.5 cm (3 in) for the hem and 5 cm (2 in) for the top fold.

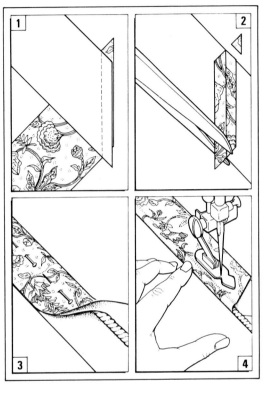

A valance should be lined, as anyone standing below can see the back of it. If you decide to make a valance with a shaped edge the lining becomes part of the overall design and should be chosen with this in mind. Interlining will give added body.

Make up a valance following the instructions for interlined or lined curtains on pages 109-112.

PIPING

Piping is used mainly for edging pelmets and tiebacks but can also be used to good effect on a curtain itself to edge both sides of an appliquéd border and as a trimming for blinds. Decide first what thickness of piping cord you want, depending on the fabric you are using and the size of the piece you are piping. Piping for soft furnishings comes in fine, medium and coarse thicknesses but for delicate fabrics and small curtains you may prefer to use a finer dressmaker's piping cord. If you are not sure of the final effect ask in the shop if you can see the different thicknesses made up.

Most piping cord is pre-shrunk but this is something you should check, especially with the cotton type, since if it shrinks during washing or cleaning you will get a puckered effect. To shrink your own piping cord put it into boiling water for about five minutes. Dry thoroughly before making up.

Fabric to cover piping cord should always be cut on the bias. To find this take a piece of the piping fabric and fold over a corner until the cut edge lies parallel with the selvedge. Press along the fold, open up the fabric and cut along the crease. Now cut parallel strips of the required fabric until you have enough, including seam allowances, to cover the necessary length of cord. The width of each strip should enclose the cord plus 1.9 cm (¾ in) and the seam allowance for joining the strips should be 10 mm (⅜ in) at each end. Join up all the strips, stitching along the straight grain of the fabric and securing both ends of the thread securely. Press open the seams and trim off the little triangles of fabric which protrude from the straight run.

With wrong sides together, fold the strip in half lengthways and insert the piping cord. Pin, tack and stitch into position as close to the cord as possible. Use the zip foot on your sewing machine.

117

ABOVE: *(1) Make up piping cord by joining strips of fabric cut on the cross. (2) Trim off surplus fabric. (3) Pin cord into position on fabric strip. (4) Using a zip foot, machine as near to cord as possible.*

The piped cord is now ready to be attached to the main fabric. If it is to trim a pelmet or tie-back you should hand stitch it along the edge and trim the ends so they do not show, or enclose them under the lining. An attractive finish is produced with a double row of piping stitched one above the other. If piping is on the face fabric of a curtain it should again be hand stitched into place with the raw ends tucked under the appliquéd border.

MAKING CAFE CURTAINS

Café curtains are not just designed to conceal a restaurant's eating customers from the gaze of the outside world. They are also useful in domestic situations where you want to exclude an unattractive view or divide one internal area from another. Depending on the fabric used they can look equally good from both sides.

Café curtains tend to be fairly short and can be used in rows of two or three sets with the facility of being drawn separately. They can also be used in conjunction with other types of curtain or blinds or instead of sheers to cover just the bottom part of the window.

Although they can be hung on any type of track or pole, café curtains, especially when hung as a single row, tend to be hung on poles with their headings an integral decorative feature. Because of this, they must be made from a fabric which is fairly close woven and unlikely to sag under its own weight. Felt is a very good choice for this type of curtain as it does not fray so needs no hems or side seams and a tab or scalloped heading can be cut directly without the need for turnings.

To make café curtains with a tab heading, cut and join the fabric to make one and a half times the width of the window and, if desired, line it as described on page 111. Do not attach the lining to the face fabric along the top of the curtain.

Decide how many tabs you want (there should be one at each end with the remainder spaced evenly between them) and mark their positions with pins. Measure round the pole to see how long they need to be and allow some extra length so that the tab effect will be visible when the curtains are drawn. Cut strips of fabric to the length of each loop plus 1.25 cm (½ in) and twice the width plus 2.5 cm (1 in). Fold each in half, right sides together and tack and stitch along the long side leaving the ends open. Turn the right way out and press so that the seam is in the centre of the tab.

If the curtain is lined press the heading allowance of both face fabric and lining so that the raw edges are inside the curtain. Place the tabs on the marked positions and pin and tack into place. If the curtain is unlined press the raw edge in and then press over the heading allowance. Press in the raw edges at each end of the tabs then pin and tack them into position. For both types of curtain now machine stitch along the top edge of the curtain so that both ends of each tab are firmly fixed. The curtain is now ready to hang.

To make café curtains with a plain scalloped heading you will need face fabric which is one and a half times the width of the window. To ensure that the scallops are even you need to make a paper or stiff card template. Prepare a strip of paper about 15 cm (6 in) deep and the same width as the made up face fabric and fold it in half. Work out how many scallops you can get along the length allowing about 3.75 cm (1½ in) between each. Using a pair of compasses, draw a half scallop at the centrefold and then work along to the end of the template, leaving at least 3.75 cm (1½ in) at the end. Cut out the scallops and open up the paper.

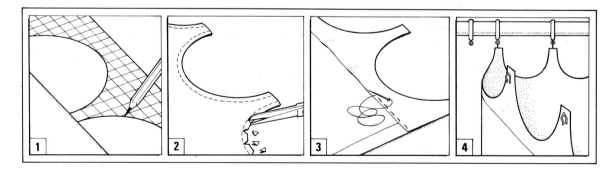

ABOVE: *When making café curtains it is important to get the scallops even. (1) Mark out the lining fabric. (2) Snip the curves to prevent puckering. (3) Stitch into position. (4) Hang from rings for an open effect.*

RIGHT: *Highly atmospheric and entirely French, the casual charm of sheer café curtains veiling long French windows, but with a space at the top through which one glimpses trees.*

Lay out the face fabric right side up and turn over the top to a depth of the scallops plus a hem allowance of 7.5 cm (3 in). Stitch down the sides. You should now have mainly right side but the fold of wrong side fabric facing you. Pin the template along the top of the fold and mark the scallops out using tailor's chalk. Remove the template and pin, tack and stitch along the markings. Cut out the scallops, leaving a fabric allowance of 1.25 cm (½ in) from the stitch line. With sharp scissors nick round the curves to prevent puckering. Turn the scallops right side out and press carefully. Slip-stitch along the hem allowance of the turning.

To hang the curtains, either sew rings along the edge beween the scallops or stitch hooks to the back of each piece of fabric between the scallops, depending on what type of track you are using.

—— CHOOSING AND MAKING NET CURTAINS ——

Net, lace and sheer curtains have lost their peeping spinster's image over the years and are now seen as an attractive and fashionable form of window treatment. You may choose to hang them simply to enhance the appearance of your window, or to obtain privacy from passers by, or to shut out an unattractive view. Net curtains, in spite of their apparent flimsiness, also offer some degree of insulation, protect carpets and furniture from strong sunlight and act as a filter for dust and dirt which come in when windows are open.

Traditionally, net and lace curtains were made from loose woven or lace design cotton and these fabrics are still popular. Their advantages are a lack of static and an ability to drape well. However, cotton does tend to be expensive, shrink when washed, need ironing to look good and is susceptible to damp, so it is not suitable for a room which suffers from condensation or is very steamy, for example a bathroom or kitchen. Man-made fibres are usually cheaper and easier to care for and come in a good range of weights and designs.

One particular net fabric is specifically designed to offer extra advantages. Verosol looks similar to plain voile but is coated with a fine layer of aluminium which allows you to see out but prevents those outside looking in. It also acts as an insulator, reducing the escape of heat from a room during winter and restricting the entry of strong sunlight during summer. It is considerably more

120

RIGHT: *It could almost be a room set from* La Traviata, *but in fact it is a solid English bay window given the diva treatment with cascades of old lace, velvet swags, silk shawls, draped tables and even a bird cage in curly wire.*

expensive than other net curtain fabrics, comes in plain and a range of colours and needs to be ordered specially. It is easily made up, drapes well but needs regular dusting to keep it clean and must be dry cleaned rather than washed.

Ready-made nets and sheers are the easy, lazy answer to dressing a window provided you can find a suitably sized design that you like. They come with side seams, hems and slotted headings already sewn and are ready to hang immediately. Ready-made nets and sheers may be plain voiles, patterned, come with frills and/or tie-backs and are also sold in crossover and jardinière form.

Semi ready-made nets come in two forms. *Long net* is sold by the metre in different widths and is usually hemmed, the hem often forming part of the design. You have to turn the side seams and stitch the heading, depending on what type of gathers you want. *Brise-bise* is also sold by the metre with a ready stitched hem, often lightly weighted to improve the drape. It also has the heading ready sewn, either as a pocket for a wire or rod or with eyelets for use on a cafe curtain rod. If you cannot buy brise-bise curtaining in the right length for your window it is best to alter the heading rather than the hem to keep the design looking good.

When choosing unprepared fabric for net curtains check that it is in fact sheer enough to allow the amount of light you want to filter through. Ask to see the fabric draped vertically and ruched up against a window before you decide. Remember too that the fabric should create a harmonious effect with your main curtain or blind fabric, wall-

covering, paint and other furnishings in the room. Some designs, especially embroidered ones, do not look nearly as good when gathered and you might get a better effect with something plainer or choose to settle for a less full effect in order to allow the pattern to show to its best advantage.

If you plan to have an unusual draped effect again consider carefully whether you want a patterned fabric. Crossover nets can cut out a lot of light if the fabric is too dense, forming a darker triangle at the area where the two curtains cross. It is also essential to ensure that the point where the curtains cross is exactly where you want it, usually the centre of the window unless you are aiming for a particular asymmetrical effect. In any case you will need two wires, rods or tracks on which to hang the two curtains.

A jardinière effect is designed to allow you to display houseplants or ornaments on a window-sill. If you do not buy this ready-made you will need to take time and trouble making it yourself since achieving an even edge is difficult, whether you go for a straight or curved effect. Beware of ending up with a curtain which is too short or it will look as if it has shrunk; if it has indeed shrunk you will end up with a very skimpy effect indeed.

The majority of sheer net curtaining sold is white although you can buy some colours. Otherwise you can dye it to any shade you want. Remember that if the curtains are to be drawn across the window during the day you will get the glow from your chosen colour in the room. White, cream and ecru curtains only look good if kept

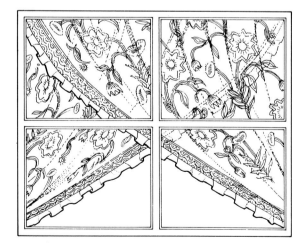

122

ABOVE RIGHT: *Sheer curtains made with a jardinière effect. They are cut in a graduated curve to display objects on the window-sill.*
ABOVE LEFT: *Crossover nets must be hung carefully so that the crossing point occurs in the centre of the window.*

COVER UPS

scrupulously clean. In a home where there are smokers these shades tend to pick up nicotine staining, so will need cleaning more often.

QUANTITY GUIDE

Net curtaining is sold in a number of ways and widths. It is worth taking a good look at what is around since with sheer fabrics you want to avoid vertical seams in the middle of the window where they stand out very obviously.

Because of their flimsy nature, net curtains can look skimpy if they are not full enough so if price is a deciding factor it is better to go for more of a cheaper fabric than less of an expensive one.

Plain nets ideally need two and a half to three times the final width of the window. This will give

fullness and show off the effect of whatever heading you choose.

Patterned nets should be about twice the width of the window. Use less and you will not get a gathered effect; use more and you will obscure the pattern itself.

When it comes to length, assuming you are not going for a crossover or jardinière effect, you should hang short net curtains so that they do not touch the window-sill. Net acts as a wick for any condensation and will quickly become rotten or covered with mildew. When hung to floor length the curtains should fall just short of the ground and they should be hemmed clear of any long pile carpet or rug which could interfere with the way they drape.

123

ABOVE: *Window compositions like this one from Reykjavik, Iceland, are a neglected form of folk art. Lacy swags and a small curtain frame the traditional pot plant; it all tells the interested observer a great deal about the household within.*

HEADING UP

Because the essence of net curtains is their sheerness, it is important not to use a heading tape or buckram which would create a thick, impenetrable band. Standard curtain tape can be used where the top of the net will be covered by a pelmet or valance; otherwise use a special tape designed to produce very small gathers (particularly suitable for small windows) or a deep, sheer pencil pleat tape especially designed for net curtains which allows you to hang them either from standard hooks or along a rod or wire. Bear in mind that if you choose other types of heading you may need to adjust the amount of fabric needed.

HANGING MATTERS

How you hang your net curtains will depend on the final effect you want at your window.

Track produces the most sophisticated effect and if correctly fitted will not develop the sagging which can occur with wire. Double and triple curtain tracks allow you to hang nets and main curtains together, with one or more sets corded.

Rods for net curtains come in two types. Spring tension rods contain an internal spring which allows each end to be braced against the walls of the window embrasure provided they are deep enough. These have the advantage of allowing you to hang the curtains at whatever height you want and as near to or far away from the glass as the depth of the recess permits. These rods are oval shaped, come only in white in widths up to 1.8 m (72 in) and do not sag.

Adjustable rods consist of an inner and outer tube which slide to adjust to the length required. Each end of the rod is screwed to the window frame (or fixed by adhesive hooks to metal and pvc frames). The maximum width possible is 3 m (120 in) and this type of rod is thicker in its longer lengths to prevent sagging. With these rods you also need to adjust the end of the curtain heading to cover the fixings.

Net wire is the traditional and cheapest method of hanging net curtains and just involves screwing two hooks at either side of the window to support a piece of plastic-coated wire into which two eyes are fixed. The maximum width possible is 2.7 m (108 in) but this is likely to sag and will need extra supporting hooks fixed along its length which tend to spoil the appearance. This type of wire has an allowance of up to 10% expansion to enable you to pull it taut but even on short lengths will tend to sag with time and need to be cut and re-adjusted. To do this you need a sharp pair of wire cutters.

Net curtains which remain in position all the time can look effective if fixed on wires or rods at both the top and the bottom. This allows you to arrange the gathers as you want them and they will remain set, not billowing if the window is opened.

CARE OF NET CURTAINS

Net curtains are the front line of fire when it comes to dust and dirt entering a window, so their open weave tends to become clogged up fairly quickly. As a general rule, especially with old lace, net curtains are best washed by hand. If you must use a machine, put them in a pillow case or underwear bag to prevent the loose weave becoming damaged by the agitation of the drum.

When hand washing, use a warm solution of soap flakes or mild detergent. Very badly soiled nets should be soaked in cold water or biological detergent before washing. Rinse thoroughly and give a final cold rinse to crisp them up. Do not spin but drip dry and rehang as soon as water has finished dripping out; in this way the curtains can dry into their folds and will not need ironing. If your net curtains become stained or soiled with smoke there are specialist whitening products on the market which can restore whiteness, although these are not suitable for coloured fabrics.

─────── CHOOSING A BLIND ───────

Blinds can be used instead of or in conjunction with curtains. They require considerably less fabric than even the least gathered curtains and in many instances are a more practical choice. For example, in kitchens and bathrooms where space is limited or where gathered curtains could create a hazard blinds are a good choice and can be made from specially treated fabrics which resist moisture and dirt. Special effect blinds such as Roman or Austrian create an attractive look at the top of a window while leaving most of the frame visible – good if you have an architecturally attractive or specially decorated frame, while festoon blinds can be left in the down or half-down position to keep out blinding sunlight or hide an unattractive vista. Used in conjunction with curtains, blinds can

125

LEFT: *More effortless, and unmistakably French, romanticism. This beguiling window-nook draws on the proven charm of lace, old lace especially, combined with a shaped pelmet, cushions and a personal medley of little prints and photographs.*

create interesting decorative effects by careful mixture of fabrics and colours. In small areas where bulky curtains would be out of proportion, a pair of pleated curtains can be used to decorate the sides of a window while a blind performs the function of covering the window when required.

Blinds may also be needed to keep out light and protect furniture or furnishings. This was in fact their original function and the fabric used for this – holland – is still available today.

Venetian blinds go in and out of vogue. They consist of horizontal slats so strung that they can be adjusted between a completely closed position where no light comes through and one where the slats lie horizontally and allow light to filter in between them. Venetian blinds come in a range of colours and are usually plastic although wooden ones can be bought or made specially. Since they act as dust traps they need careful cleaning; you can buy a specially shaped brush which slides between the slats.

Vertical blinds which work in the same way as Venetian blinds produce a similar effect but are usually made of treated fabric or plastic.

Pinoleum blinds are made of slatted wood and come in a wide range of colours and sizes. They are sold either as straightforward roller blinds or as Roman blinds. They are good for keeping out sun but are not totally light proof. They are a good choice for sun rooms and conservatories and go especially well with cane and rattan furniture.

BUYING BLINDS

While you can buy ready-made blinds, they tend to be of the easy-clean type suitable for use in kitchens or bathrooms. There is a reasonably good choice of colours and designs but if you want a particular effect you will usually have to have it specially made or make it yourself. In any case, make sure you measure up accurately so that the finished blind is the right size. Ideally, get a second person to check your measurements.

Check where the blind will be fitted as this may affect the type you choose. Roller blinds can be fixed at the sides of a window, from the top of it or on the face of the frame. Gathered blinds such as Austrian, festoon and Roman need to be hung from a batten running along the top of the window.

Roller blinds require a firm, evenly woven fabric that will hold its shape and can be stiffened if

126

RIGHT: *Michael and Patti Hopkins are two architects who really do live in a glass box, designed and built by them in a leafy street in Hampstead. Glare and overheating, glass box hazards, are controlled and modified by Venetian blinds everywhere, which can be raised, lowered, or opened up, according to the weather.*

necessary. Austrian and Roman blinds also require an even weave but the weight of the fabric will depend on the final effect required. Festoon blinds should be made of light fabric which will drape well.

——— ROLLER BLINDS ———

Roller blinds can be bought in kit form virtually ready-made. You just cut the pole and batten to the correct widths for the window, fix on the spring and metal caps supplied and attach the fabric. Some manufacturers of these kits supply touch and close fastening which you fix with adhesive to the pole and the fabric and then join together: others require you to fix the fabric to the pole with tacks or staples which you may have to supply yourself. In some instances the fabric supplied in a blind kit may come ready-treated; otherwise you will have to do this yourself, using a commercial aerosol (see page 130).

If you want to provide your own fabric you can buy the basic kit, cut it and your chosen material to size and make up as above. When cutting fabric either supplied with or purchased for a kit, take great care to make sure that it hangs straight. Check the pattern in relation to the selvedges before you start to cut and use a T-square or set square and long rigid ruler to mark the cutting lines. Double check before you cut.

Fabric should be cut to the same length as the roller and about 15 cm (6 in) longer than the final drop. Side hems should be kept to just one turning and, depending on the type of fabric, you may be able to fix them with fabric adhesive or an iron-on double sided adhesive interlining. You should also avoid making the hem bulky.

The bottom edge of a roller blind offers considerable scope for decoration. You can make a shaped edge to fix to the bottom, using a template in the same way as when making pelmets. You can attach a trimming such as braid or fringing or cover the pocket holding the wooden batten with a strip of contrasting or toning fabric.

Ready-made kits have a pocket formed at the base of the blind fabric through which you slip the batten and then attach the acorn supplied. Most of the cording and acorns supplied with blind-making kits tend to be cheap and nasty. It is also worth noting that white cord rapidly becomes dirty in areas such as kitchens while plastic acorns are often poor quality that does not stand up to repeated pulling. You can buy both cord and acorns separately from specialist curtain and trimming stores which should have a good selection to choose from.

STENCILLING
Stencilling your own design on to a plain fabric is an excellent way of creating an original blind and a method that can be used to allow you to pick up a motif from a wallcovering or favourite picture in the room.

Before stencilling, cut the fabric to size and prepare it with its side and bottom hems so that you can see where to position the design.

Fix the fabric to a flat surface using fine-headed drawing pins or thick masking tape and fix your cut stencil in position using masking tape. You will need a stencil brush (from art shops) and a set of fabric paints. Follow the instructions supplied for using these and take care that the fabric on which you are working can stand the recommended ironing temperature used to fix the colour. Do not

129

LEFT: *Venetian blinds soften incoming light as efficiently as the most swooning lace, and their brisk functionalism suits interiors with a mainly contemporary feel, such as this dining room belonging to Barbara Smallhouse.*

ABOVE: *A clown's face, made up entirely of coloured beads, is a perfect cover-up for a tiny window and makes teeth brushing more fun in this child's bedroom.*

apply fabric stiffener or dirt repellent until the stencilled pattern is completely dry.

STIFFENING A BLIND

If you do not use ready stiffened fabric, you will need to apply a stiffener yourself. This should be done before the blind is made up. Note that stiffening may cause the fabric to shrink so do not cut the fabric to size until stiffening has been completed and check the dimensions after it has dried. Some blind kits come supplied with a sufficient quantity of stiffener; with others you need to buy it separately.

Soak-type stiffener is easy to use. You make up the solution and soak the fabric for the specified time. After this it must be hung up so that it can drip dry without forming creases. Iron while still damp until it is bone dry to set the stiffening.

Aerosol spray stiffeners can be applied to the fabric before or after making up. Again you must be able to hang the fabric up and it is best, if possible, to work outdoors since this type of chemical gives off unpleasant fumes. Choose a day when there is no wind and pick a draught-free spot. If you have to work indoors, open all the windows and wear a nose and face mask to prevent breathing in fumes.

ROMAN BLINDS

Unlike roller blinds, Roman blinds pull up in soft rectangular folds, producing a horizontal pleated effect at the top of the window and a flat covering when down. They take little more fabric than the surface area to be covered requires but need to be lined and possibly interlined for a more insulated effect. They can also be quilted, either by using a quilted fabric in the first place or by quilting your own to a design of your choice.

Roman blinds should be made from a firmly woven curtain or upholstery weight fabric that will not lose its shape. You do not need to use a commercial stiffener for Roman blinds but may wish to apply an aerosol dirt repellent depending on where the blind is to be sited.

For very wide windows it is better to make more than one blind, rather than join several widths of fabric. If you do need to make a join remember that it is always best to have a whole width of fabric in the centre of a blind and a half width on either

side. Try to ensure that the seam lines are where drops of the backing tape are fixed.

You can buy a Roman blind kit which contains everything needed to make one apart from the wall-fixing batten used at the top. Otherwise you will need to buy special Roman blind tape or standard curtain heading tape or 2.5 cm (1 in) wide cotton tape. With standard curtain tape you should use 12 mm (½ in) split brass rings that can be slid in to position the gathers and with cotton tape you will need 12 mm (½ in) diameter brass rings. You will also need nylon cord to run through the rings, a securing cleat, a batten of 25 × 12 mm (1 × 1½ in) wood cut to the width of the blind to weight it down and a length of timber 50 × 25 mm (2 × 1 in) to fix it to the wall or top of the window embrasure.

For the top of the blind you will need a screw eye for the top of each vertical tape to fix it to the wall batten and one larger screw eye through which all the cords will run at the side of the window. Use tacks or a staple gun to fix the blind fabric to the wall batten.

MAKING UP

Cut fabric, lining and interlining, if used, to the size of the area to be covered, allowing 15.5 cm (7 in) for top and bottom turnings and 7.5 cm (3 in) for side hems. If the blind is very wide you will need to interlock the fabrics together as if making lined curtains (see page 112). With wrong sides together stitch round the blind with a 12 mm (½ in) seam allowance, leaving a 5 cm (2 in) gap unstitched 2.5 cm (1 in) from the bottom edge to allow you to insert the batten and also leaving a gap large enough to allow you to turn the 'bag' you have made the right way out. Press the seams to the centre, turn right way out and press again. Stitch up the gap left for turning and sew two parallel rows of stitching 5 cm (2 in) apart along the edges of the gap left for the batten. Insert the batten and stitch up the ends.

Cut the tape into lengths measuring from the top of the blind to the top of the batten pocket. You will need one tape at each side and enough tape to run at roughly 25-30 cm (10-12 in) across the blind at evenly spaced intervals. Pin or tack into position and stitch down both sides of each tape, starting 6 cm (2½ in) from the top and working through all the thicknesses of the fabric.

With tailor's chalk or pins, mark the positions

for the ring fixings along each length of tape. Remember that the distance between the rings will decide the depth of the concertina folds when the blind is in the up position. It is vital that each horizontal row of rings is parallel to each other and to the top and bottom edges of the blind. If you are using whole rings, sew them firmly on the marked spots; split rings can be inserted into the appropriate holes if you are using standard gathered curtain tape. Turn down the top of the blind 2.5 cm (1 in) and stitch firmly.

Lay the blind out flat with the top heading along the wall-fixing batten. Tack or staple it along the top edge of the batten. Insert the screw eyes along the bottom edge of the wall fixing so that they are in line with the rows of tape. Decide on which side you want the blind to pull up and fix the large screw eye at that end.

Cut lengths of nylon cord to run through the rows of rings and along the screw eyes to the larger one. Each cord length will be different, with the longest being the one which starts diagonally opposite the larger screw eye. Knot each length of cord firmly to the bottom ring on each row before threading it up.

Pull the blind into the drawn position while still lying flat and cover it with a piece of chipboard or hardboard weighted down with books. Leave for two or three days to allow the pleats to set firmly into position.

Screw the wall-fixing batten into position over the window. Fix the cleat on the left or right hand side as previously decided. Lower the blind into the down position and check that all the cords are a suitable length to be wound round the cleat before trimming them so that they reach an even finish.

Roman blinds can be decorated in a number of ways. You can appliqué braid down the sides or across the pleats or make a shaped bottom edge (see also pelmets and roller blinds).

Austrian and Festoon Blinds

Austrian and festoon blinds are frequently confused, one for the other. In fact, an Austrian blind is a pull-up curtain, similar in some respects to a Roman blind. In the down position it forms a flat covering for the window surface but when pulled up it is ruched vertically and pleated horizontally.

A festoon blind is made in a similar way but uses considerably more fabric and remains ruched whether in the up or down position. Some festoon blinds are left permanently down to cover windows in the same way as net curtains; others are pulled up and down as required. While an Austrian blind can be pulled up to reveal most of the window and

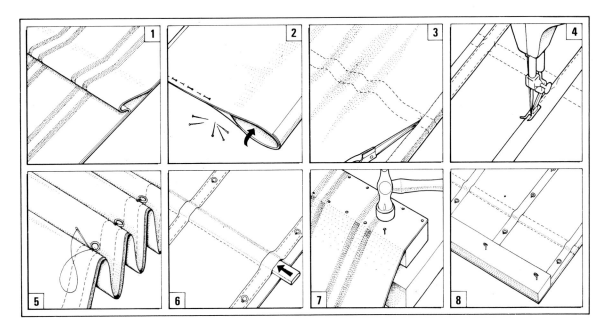

Assembling a Roman blind. (1) Match up blind and lining edges. (2) Turn edges in neatly and evenly. (3) Separate lining so you can insert batten at one end of channel. (4) Stitch down vertical tapes, avoiding batten channel. (5) Attach rings if not using tape already fitted with them. (6) Slide batten into channel. (7) Straighten fabric and attach to batten with panel pins. (8) Insert a screw eye into the batten at the top of each vertical tape.

its frame, a festoon blind, because of the bulk of fabric it takes, will always cover at least one third of the window.

An Austrian blind can be made of any fabric which drapes well and is suitable for curtains, although it needs to be a fairly firm weave so that it will hold its shape. A festoon blind is best made of light, flimsy fabric since because of the quantity required a firm fabric would result in unsightly bulkiness at the top of the window when drawn up.

Both types require more fabric than roller or Roman blinds since in addition to being ruched horizontally, they are also gathered vertically. Austrian blinds are usually lined but festoons drape more satisfactorily if they are not.

You can buy special kits which contain all the items needed for making Austrian and festoon blinds. Some include the curtain track but others do not. The blinds can be made in the same way as Roman blinds, using special Austrian/festoon blind tape which is designed in a similar way to curtain heading with cords that pull up vertically, or using cotton tape to which you attach rings.

To enhance their ruched effect, many Austrian blinds have a frill at the bottom and sometimes down the side edges as well. If you decide to add frills you must work out how deep they should be in relation to the total area of the blind and allow for this when buying the fabric.

MAKING UP

First, cut out the fabric. For an Austrian blind this should be calculated as twice the width of the area to be covered and the depth plus 17.5 cm (7 in) (to allow for hems). If you have to join drops of fabric, remember that a blind looks best with one central panel and two half widths, one at each side. Try to ensure that the vertical tapes coincide with any seams.

If you want to line an Austrian blind, cut the lining fabric to the same size as the face fabric and lay them right sides together. Tack, pin and machine round the sides and top, turn right sides out and press into shape. There is no need to lock the fabrics together as when making curtains as the vertical tapes will prevent the lining billowing away from the face fabric.

For unlined blinds, make 12 mm (½ in) seams down the sides, press a 12 mm (½ in) seam along the top of the blind fabric. Tack and machine stitch your chosen curtain heading into position. With pins or tailor's chalk, mark the position of the vertical tapes. These should be positioned along each edge and at approximately 25-50 cm (10-20 in) apart, depending on the width of the window and how full you want each swag to look when ruched up. Make sure that the vertical tapes are parallel and, if using commercial Austrian blind tape, that the gathering points lie parallel horizontally. Stitch down both sides of each tape.

If you are using ready-corded Austrian/festoon blind tape this can just be pulled up when required. Otherwise you will need to sew on brass rings or insert split ones into the tape (see Roman blinds, page 131). If you are using rings you will need to insert nylon cord as for Roman blinds. Before pulling up the blind you should either hem it or attach the frill.

To make a frill, cut a strip of fabric two to two

ABOVE: *Making up an Austrian blind. (1) Fix the frill and attach the vertical corded tapes. (2) Pull up the horizontal tape. (3) Attach to track using standard curtain hooks. (4) Drawing into position.*

RIGHT: *Shamelessly feminine frou-frou, all pastel chintz, lace trimmed festoon blinds and blurry flower prints, in the delicious bedroom of designer Tricia Guild.*

132

and a half times the width of the bottom and, if required, the length of the sides. It should be the finished depth of the frill plus 3.75 cm (1½ in). Make a double 6 mm (¼ in) hem along the long edge and two short ends unless you are planning to frill all three sides, in which case hem only one short end of the sides and neither on the base frill. Sew two parallel rows of gathering stitches, 6 mm (¼ in) apart, along the long edges and draw up the frills to their finished lengths, fastening off both threads firmly. Pin and tack to the wrong side of the blind and machine stitch into position. When you have attached both side and base frills, adjust the unhemmed short ends correctly and slip stitch into position.

For a more tailored effect you can make a box-pleated frill to edge an Austrian blind. Decide on the size and distance apart of the pleats and cut the fabric accordingly. Hem, then tack and press the pleats into position. Machine stitch into position on the blind.

Cut a piece of timber 50×25 mm (2×1 in) to the width of the window and fix to it a piece of the appropriate curtain track for the heading tape. Screw into position at the top of the window frame and, using the correct curtain hooks, put the blind into position. Fix a cleat on the side you want to draw up the cords and cut them to even lengths when you have allowed enough to let the blind be raised and lowered.

—— FESTOON BLINDS ——

Festoon blinds are made in the same way as Austrian ones but without lining or frills. They should be two to two and a half times the drop of the window and twice the width. They tend to be more fiddly to make than Austrian blinds because of the volume of fabric which also tends to be flimsy and therefore slippery.

—— MAKING FRILLS ——

For a gathered frill you need a piece of fabric between one and a half and two times the final width required. The depth will depend on the size of the main piece of fabric being frilled.

Join the short edges of the fabric and press the seams open. Where the frill is to be longer than about 90 cm (36 in) make up the frills separately and join them when gathering and hemming is completed.

Either hem the frill, turning in the raw edge and then turning a 12 mm (½ in) allowance or cut twice the depth of fabric and fold, wrong sides together, and press along the fold line. Use a long straight stitch on a sewing machine or gather stitch by hand and fasten the threads at both ends securely, when you have pulled the frill up to the required length. If a long frill is being made, this is the stage at which to join the various gathered lengths.

Now, with right sides together, pin, tack and stitch the frill to the curtain or blind, making sure that the gathers are evenly spaced before you do the final machining. If the frill is to go round corners on a blind or curtain allow slightly more fullness at these points.

When making a box pleated frill allow at least three times the length of the area to be frilled depending on the size of the pleats. Measure the points to be pleated and mark them with pins. Pin into position, tack and press. Pin, tack and stitch on to the face fabric.

—— EXTERNAL BLINDS ——

External blinds may be needed for practical purposes or purely to enhance the outside appearance of a house. They may be essential for protecting furnishings from sunlight which causes fading or for keeping the refrigerator and freezer in a sunny kitchen cool. Because they need to stand up to winter as well as summer weather they are items which are best made professionally from properly treated material which will not rot or be damaged by sun, rain or snow. It should not be hard to track down a supplier who will custom make to your specification; most firms in this line of business also deal with commercial outlets such as restaurants where each job is a one-off in terms of size.

You must decide whether you want to be able to open and close your external blind or whether it is to act as a permanent canopy over a window. With the former type you should check what the blind looks like in the closed position; some retract neatly into a box, just leaving a small valance showing, while others pleat up into a less tailored shape. It is even possible to obtain huge awnings which pull out to form a tent effect and produce a covered area outside.

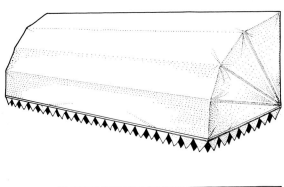

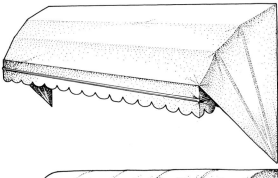

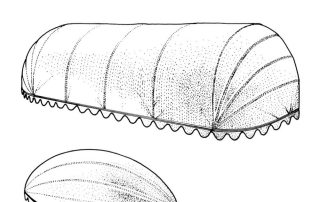

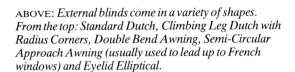

ABOVE: *External blinds come in a variety of shapes. From the top: Standard Dutch, Climbing Leg Dutch with Radius Corners, Double Bend Awning, Semi-Circular Approach Awning (usually used to lead up to French windows) and Eyelid Elliptical.*

COVER UPS

Suit the blind to the external decor of your home. A rural cottage will be spoiled with a high-tech awning while an uncompromisingly modern high-rise balcony can take a tailored rather than a soft look. The illustrations show the various shapes available.

Check the mechanism for raising and lowering your chosen blind. It should be easy to operate and made of a material which will not be damaged by weather. Note that some large blinds may need two people to operate them.

--- **WINDOW SEATS** ---

Where a window looks out on a marvellous view or is sited in the kind of alcove that calls for someone to curl up in it, a window seat may be a good decorative feature. It is not advisable to site a window seat over a radiator, since you will then be paying good money to heat the occasional bottom but not the rest of the room. A window seat built into a window embrasure will allow you to draw full length curtains across it at night. Otherwise your curtains should come down to the window seat but not trail on it.

Because a window seat is a fairly simple structure it is easy to make yourself or you could get a carpenter to make the base and upholster it yourself. For the base you will need chipboard, cut to the size of the final window seat. To support it you can either fix it to the wall using very strong shelf brackets and put legs (available ready cut from do-it-yourself shops) or another piece of chipboard to support the front edge. Or you can use legs to support it all the way round. If you are making a window seat to go round a bay it may be easier to make the base in more than one piece; this will depend on the size and shape.

Alternatively, you may prefer to buy an inexpensive blanket chest or children's toy box of a suitable size and upholster the top so it acts as a window seat while still functioning as a storage unit. If you are using a chest that was not originally intended as a seat check that it is strong enough to act as one.

The height of the window seat should enable people to sit comfortably and look out of it; there is no need to have it at sill height unless this is what the aesthetics of the room dictate.

To upholster a window seat you need to use

135

medium grade foam rubber not less than 7.5 cm (3 in) deep and deeper if you want a more padded effect. Ideally, get the supplier to cut the foam rubber to size since this is a task which is much easier using specialist equipment. If you have to do it yourself buy or borrow an electric carving knife which will cut more quickly and straight than if you attempt to do it with an ordinary knife or long-bladed scissors. Decide whether you want one large cushion or two or three smaller ones. If the seat runs round a bay you will not be able to upholster it in one piece.

The fabric to cover it should be upholstery weight. Using the cut foam as a guide, make paper pattern pieces for the six sides of each cushion. You could economise by choosing curtain lining or other inexpensive fabric for the underside of the cushions but will get more wear out of them if you can turn them over. This may not be possible with cushions cut to fit unusual sized bays and alcoves.

Tailored shapes such as these look good if piped and this also strengthens the seams and prevents wear on them. If you plan to pipe you will need to make up appropriate lengths of covered piping cord (see page 117) before you start putting the fabric pieces together. Cut the fabric pieces, allowing 1.25 cm ($\frac{1}{2}$ in) seam allowance all round. Decide if you want to be able to remove the fabric covers for washing or cleaning and if so you will need to allow for this. Use Velcro or continuous popper tape and buy enough to run the opening along one and a half sides; with a rectangular cushion run it halfway along the bottom back edge and along one of the short bottom side edges.

Pin, tack and machine stitch the pieces together with the piping if used. Turn the right way out, press and put over the foam pieces. Note that you cannot press the pieces once they are on the foam as the heat of the iron could damage it.

To cover the front and sides of the window seat make a valance following the instructions on page 117. This type of valance does not need to be lined. You can either fix it to the edge of the window seat with drawing pins or touch and close fastening or you can attach the pleated valance to a piece of fabric to go over the top of the base and under the foam cushion.

MAKING A FABRIC SHUTTER

The light, airy shutters shown opposite provide an unusual form of window treatment. In this case they merely shade the window and afford some privacy, but made up in a thicker material they would also exclude light.

To make the basic frames for the shutters you will need enough timber of 50 mm × 25 mm (2 × 1 in) width softwood to make as many four-sided frames as you need for the shutters. Do not hinge more than two sections together or the unfixed end will sag. If the shutter frame is fairly wide it should be hinged only to the wall. If the shutters are to be more than 92 cm (36 in) high you will need to fit a strengthener bar across the middle of the frame. This should also be made of 50 mm × 25 mm (2 × 1 in) softwood.

Use simple halving joints to fit the pieces of wood to each other and secure them with wood glue and 20 mm ($\frac{3}{4}$ in) oval nails. Fix the strengthener across the centre of the shutter using halving joints and oval nails driven in at an acute angle rather than a straight one which will not fix as firmly and which may result in the nail point going right through the wood. Punch all the nail heads until they are below the wood surface and fill in the holes with plastic wood. When dry, smooth this down using fine glass paper. Paint the whole frame with a wood primer and then apply the desired finish of matt or gloss paint. Alternatively use a wood stainer to achieve the effect you want.

Cut the fabric to size; you will need a piece on each side of each frame. Allow a 1.25 cm ($\frac{1}{2}$ in) fold allowance. Press the allowance round the edge of the fabric and, using a stapler or upholstery tacks, fix the fabric as close to the pressed seam as possible round the edge of the frame, working on the underside for the top and side edges as far as you can. Finish with ornamental brass headed tacks fixed on the right side or by glueing on half-round beading or cord. To fix into position use flush hinges fixed 10 cm (4 in) from the top and bottom of the frame using countersunk wood screws. To hold the shutters together when fixed across the window fix a lightweight latch or pair of cords to the edges.

136

RIGHT Yards of cheap cotton sheeting, plus a lot of imagination, have turned that bedsit eyesore, a divan bed, into a sleeping alcove worthy of Scheherezade. The designer responsible printed the filigree design herself and used its elegant graphics to cover cushions and brilliantly improvised shutters – light, battened frames covered with fabric.

If you think of a window as a light box, with a frame, there is a lot of decorative mileage to be had from standing or hanging translucent coloured objects inside the box; incoming light will show them off in the best possible way.

Roundels of stained glass suspended inside the window frame look rich and jewel like, without giving the dim religious light which occurs when the whole window is filled with stained glass. Old pieces do sometimes turn up in junk shops, but there are contemporary versions showing flowers or dragonflies in the Tiffany style. Keen hobbyists can buy coloured glass and copper foil, and make their own.

Glass objects are another obvious choice. The best way to display these, if you have enough, is on glass shelves positioned across the window space, on small brackets so they can be taken down for cleaning. Any glass collectibles, from rare Venetian goblets to coloured glass Victorian medicine bottles, look vivid and romantic silhouetted against the light. If the window is one you leave uncurtained at night there is the added bonus of the outside view of them lit from within. Cleverly staged ideas like these have to be maintained, though, and regularly dusted, or they begin to look tacky, like a nightclub by daylight.

A scrap of lace over the window and a bushy plant on the sill is the easiest ad hoc screen for a dismal view. A fall of brilliant glass beads does the same thing in a different way. Or if the outlook really is zero, glaze the window with mirror glass – see through or opaque, and stand something pretty to reflect in it.

One or more quite large pieces of decorative glass, like the postwar Italian glass in brilliant colours which is becoming popular with collectors, might look better grouped on transparent perspex cubes of varying heights, on the window-sill. One of the best places to find new ideas for displaying favourite objects is in an up-to-date museum. Museum design is all to do with framing objects and giving them importance, in a sympathetic context. Glass beads, strung to make patterns, as they once were, really come into their own suspended across a window. Designer Edina Ronay has a pelmet of glass beads fixed across a window in her London house which doubles as a screen; the window is on the ground floor quite close to the street. Round glass beads pick up light in the most dazzling way. This is an idea which would look spectacular worked out in clear glass beads, like frozen rain. Any good hobby shop these days carries a huge stock of beads, plus the special needles and strong thread needed if you are making long danglers. Beads are astonishingly heavy in large quantities. If you are threading a long string of them, it is sensible to knot from time to time, so if one string snaps you do not have to spend hours groping about the floor. And make sure the fixing is sturdy too, and can be lifted off to clean the window panes behind.

Faceted crystal drops, rescued from defunct chandeliers, often turn up in junk shops. Strung together on knotted thread or wire, these look pretty hung in a window frame against the light, acting like tiny prisms when the sun catches them. You do not need very many and they should not be closely threaded like a necklace, just a few threaded at intervals will concentrate incoming light in a magical way. Blown glass witch balls, or the iridescent glass globes which fishermen used to

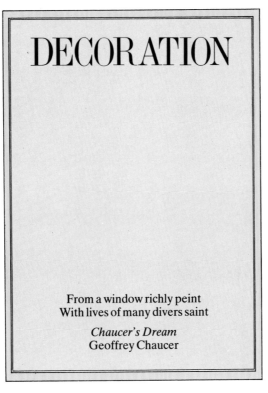

DECORATION

From a window richly peint
With lives of many divers saint

Chaucer's Dream
Geoffrey Chaucer

139

LEFT: *Oh, I do like to be beside the seaside, especially when I am really in a small dining room in Regents Park. The seaside theme comes across strongly, and gaily, in bead curtains matching striped chair seats and the mural deckchair, and lobsters are everywhere.*

use as floats, were the cottagers' version of this sort of sparkling window feature. These are less easily come by than they used to be, but if you find some when browsing through a junk shop, there is no better place for them than suspended in a small deep window, where they shimmer like perpetual Christmas decorations.

Many plants look their best back lit, and a natural screen of living green can transform a window, with benefit to the plants provided they are reasonably hardy and do not mind the window temperature dropping sharply at night. You can grow them up sticks or string, or if they are long enough to drape, loop them in swags inside the window frame, using garden wire and small hooks or eyelets to fasten them in place. Ivy is an obvious choice, good tempered in most situations and always handsome with its sharply delineated leaves, but slightly more exotic and tender climbers would do well in centrally heated conditions – plumbago, for instance, with delicate flower heads of washed

out blue and feathery foliage, jasmine, extra-ordinarily sweet scented in its flowering season. One green-bedecked window I have never forgot-ten belonged to friends, then living in London with scarcely any garden space, who trained runner beans up bamboo in front of their basement kitchen windows. The position was sunny and sheltered, and the beans responded magnificently. Washing up at the sink, one had the pleasure of watching this unlikely inner city crop race up its bamboo poles, flower and finally produce real, edible runner beans, right under their eyes. Though they now garden on a much larger scale on the south coast, I doubt whether their bean crops are ever so eagerly anticipated as they were when they scrambled up out of grow bags in the narrow ravine of a London front area.

Translucency is the obvious quality one looks for in the things one chooses to decorate a window space with, but strong incoming light also sil-houettes and heightens interesting shapes, which

ABOVE: *A roundel of coloured glass makes a vivid centrepiece in a small oval window above a wide sill which is packed with shells, dried flowers and personal bric-a-brac.*

RIGHT: *Windows make good display boxes for shapely salvage, like the frilly fretwork from a demolished hotel, and stained glass from an old house, which soften and filter the light in the bedroom of artist John Nankivell.*

ABOVE: *Decorative oddments, assembled with an eye to colour and effect, make a small room high above central London look like Tippoo Sahib's war tent. Pakistani tent hangings in vivid colours and rows of painted masks pick up the colours of embroidered cushions against a background of Indian red.*

might lose their vitality positioned on top of a piece of furniture against a wall, as most objets d'art tend to be displayed. I think there is a case for displaying small sculpture, nicely rounded or bellying pots, sea corals, indeed many of the vigorous, quirky smaller objects most magpie types accumulate over the years, in the natural light box that a suitably deep window with a generous sill provides. It is not just that the background light throws their shapes and textures into dramatic relief, but that people's eyes tend to wander towards the windows in any room, so that whatever arrangement you contrive there will be properly valued and noticed. Common sense suggests reservations here – it would be a daffy character who stood a valuable object on a cottage window-sill overlooking a busy street.

David Copperfield's aunt, the formidable Betsey Trotwood, kept a green silk fan-shaped screen sitting on her window-sill, partly to shade her as she sat sewing by the window, partly, one suspects, so that she could peer out from behind it on the watch for the promenading 'donkies' – this was nineteenth century Dover – which trampled her front garden. This suggests a possible use for other small decorative screens which get lost standing at floor level. Thirties decorative glass fire screens would be particularly effective, giving some privacy without blocking too much light. Real fans, opened out and propped on the wire mounts sold for displaying cups and saucers, would look attractive too, but choose ones that will not fade in the constant light, or cheap paper ones that can be thrown away without a qualm.

Windows are the obvious place to display the gorgeously vivid Indian embroideries, often inset with tiny mirrors, which often finish in a row of flat panels, like a pelmet. People often hang these over doors but they look better still over windows, teamed up with vivid print curtains or a simple pinoleum blind. Our photo shows how exciting ethnic embroideries look when they are used dramatically, as the top colour note in an interior stuffed with deep colours, textures and vivid bits and pieces like the row of painted masks. Nothing in this room is a collector's item, or special in itself; it is the lavish way the effects are piled up that makes it so effective and original. Because the windows in this central London apartment have a dismal view, they are screened by light-filtering blinds, with all the decorative interest going to the window treatments instead. Stagey rooms usually look best with natural light well subdued, and electric light kept low and mysterious.

One source of light which should be used more often in domestic situations is top light. The light that enters a space from above has a special, mysterious quality. It can be dramatic, or serene, practical or luxurious, but it has the charm of being unexpected. Our conditioning is so strong that walking into a room and finding it lit from overhead instead of through windows at eye level is always surprising. Windows make connections, but instead of connecting us to the world of streets, people, trees or nature, the familiar world, sky windows connect us with the cosmic mysteries, light, dark, space, the elements. Whether or not we respond to all this consciously, most top lit spaces affect us at some level as being inward turned, contemplative retreats from the bustle and challenge of every-day life. One might not wish to find this every-where in a house, but as peoples' lives get more rushed and dispersed, it could be good to have one place in a home where lighting creates a sense of self-collected tranquillity.

Overhead windows fall, roughly speaking, into two rather different categories, both of which can be traced back to ancient prototypes. The most primitive form began as a simple hole in the roof. Its primary purpose was to let smoke escape, but the small light it gave must also have been welcome in the beehive shaped dwellings, of mud plastered reeds, which are among the first known purpose built habitations. Clusters of these have been ex-cavated in the Middle East dating back to 8000 years before Christ. This type of roof aperture, primarily functional, admitting a focussed beam of light, must have been the ancestor of the classical 'oculus', or 'eye' in the roof, often a domed roof, which archi-

tects have found intriguing for its theatrical quality, like an organic spotlight. Le Corbusier's use of light shafts, focussing coloured light via stained glass on to the unadorned altars of his church of Ronchamps, is a brilliant exploitation of this property of intense, directed overhead lighting.

The other type of overhead light, or sky window, seems to have derived from a different situation, the roof open to the sky which is a feature of hot climate architecture all over the world, but was defined in the classical repertoire as an 'atrium', or courtyard open over-head; this was before glazed roofs became practical. Rich or privi-leged Romans might live in villas built on promon-tories with views in all directions, but most citizens were packed into houses along streets, as in Pompeii, where pri-vacy was of greater im-portance than views. The difference between these houses and our suburban or terrace housing is that – in common with most traditional Mediterra-nean houses to this day – an open courtyard or atrium was the centre or hub around which life revolved, whereas the street front would have been almost fortress like in its featureless, win-dowless blankness. Flooding the centre of a build-ing, or space, with natural light is highly practical in hot countries because it admits light and air to all the peripheral rooms, as well as airy shade under the colonnade or loggia in between. But it is also strangely luxurious; there is the sense of owning one's own patch of infinity, with which one is in direct contact every time one looks up.

Our second type of rooflight, which only en-tered architectural practice after the problems of glazing on a large scale had been solved by Paxton and his followers, is a conscious play upon the

SKYLIGHTS

A wise man,
Watching the stars pass across the sky,
Remarked:
In the upper air the fireflies move more slowly.

Meditation
Amy Lowell

RIGHT: *A great glass bubble of a rooflight drops real sunlight down into an extravaganza of a room, all perspex and movie stars' make-up mirrors studded with light bulbs.*

luxurious and poetic connotations of having an atrium, or roof open to the heavens. Once glazing techniques made it possible for buildings in northern climates to enjoy this illusion of greater openness, internally, many distinguished architects found the new freedom irresistible. Horta's wonderful Art Nouveau building in Brussels exploits the pearly light cast by large expanses of glazed roof. Frank Lloyd Wright's extraordinary Johnson Wax building has a huge glass roof supported on delicate concrete pillars splaying out like waterlily pads as they meet the glass, an idea he is thought to have arrived at while contemplating the waterlily pool in the Imperial Hotel in Tokyo. The Johnson Wax roof is made up of thousands of tiny glass tubes and looked at from below gives the effect of water brushed by the wind.

Tradition need not be binding upon us, but having some sense of how solutions were arrived at, and how the most original minds dramatised them, opens up more interesting options. Whether you are just looking for the cheapest way of letting overhead light into a loft or passage, or contemplating something more expansive, like turning a back yard into a big roof-glazed room, there are precedents and possibilities worth investigating.

SIMPLE SOLUTIONS

The simplest, cheapest roof lighting to install, quite adequate where extra light is the only requirement and ventilation is already taken care of, is the solution adopted by workshops and small industrial units – replacing an area of the existing roof with one of the many transparent roofing materials now available. These range from glass pantiles to corrugated acrylic sheets, and your choice here will be directed probably by the existing roof material. The idea is that the transparent material slots into the existing structure, seamlessly, so that rain runs off automatically, and no special support or framing is needed. I have roofed over a window-

ABOVE: *This London studio sitting room feels more like an attic than a basement thanks to the generous and ingenious roof lights which bring sunlight into the cool grey spaces below and a serene atmosphere.*

less passage using corrugated acrylic sheet, and it has stood up satisfactorily to the weather and looks attractive in a crude way, with the rafters exposed internally. A glorified lean-to, but light enough to make a feature of murals painted on both walls below. A neighbour, with a fine old Georgian house which only has a tiny backyard, covered in part of it with glass pantiles to make a small sheltered spot to sit in, in sunny weather. Both these are feasible DIY projects, requiring timber frame rather than the steel frame or elaborate joinery needed for proper greenhouse type glazing. In a similar way, a little light can be admitted into a loft space by substituting a sheet of wired glass for some of the slates. A sympathetic builder can tackle a job like this from inside, which cuts out the need for expensive scaffolding. This is an ad hoc solution at best, a cheap way of making a loft space usable for storage, but not really adequate if you are thinking of turning a loft into an extra room because it obviously cannot provide ventilation. Loft spaces, where all the hot air in the house collects, badly need air flowing through them to become habitable.

The traditional way to instal a window in a sloping roof space was with the dormer, which projects from the roof like a small glazed porch with its own pitched roof. Dormers have lots of advantages. They give extra headroom, sometimes necessary if a loft conversion is to obtain planning permission. They often command a splendid view, being so high up. And if the 'cheeks' are glazed, they let in as much light as a small bay window. Also, in the quirky scenery of loft rooms, their angles and nooks add charm and character and are fun to decorate with bands of stencils and cotton blinds. But they can be quite expensive, as the existing roof structure will need to be chopped about, and scaffolding put up. If you are thinking of putting in a dormer it may be worth looking into alternative types. It may not cost that much more, relatively speaking, to put in one extra long dormer window, than two small ones. But spare a thought for the look of your house and the rest of the street before rushing into ambitious roof extension schemes; the back of the house might be the best place in any case, away from street noise, and looking over gardens, especially if it also has a sunny aspect.

Terraced period houses sometimes have shal-

lowly pitched roofs behind a parapet wall. To make their roof space into anything like a room the roof usually has to be raised a few feet, and the usual practice is to install a long window running along behind the parapet. If the window is set back a yard or so from the parapet, the whole roof can be raised quite a bit higher than its neighbours without being conspicuous from below. In the case of listed houses a scheme like this is probably the only one which might get planning approval. Where the roof area is really sizeable, it may even be possible to combine a roof extension with a small roof garden.

None of these ideas are cheap, though they can work out a lot cheaper than buying a larger house if you are pressed for space. But there are now greatly improved, weathertight rooflights available, mostly in aluminium, which provide a cheap way of introducing a window which can be opened and closed into a pitched roof without going to the expense of dormers. In some situations, these are the best looking, as well as the most economical, solution. In an old barn, for instance, or indeed any old building with a distinctive pitched roof which would be spoilt by an outcrop of dormers. They can be installed where they are most needed, in a regular pattern, or more dramatically, in a sort of scatter arrangement to make a chequerboard of light seen from below. Used like this, skylights are as much decorative as functional. Setting small windows into a large expanse of roof or wall can look very dramatic, as Le Corbusier's Ronchamps church demonstrated, with its irregular cluster of small free form windows set like chinks of coloured light into a slab of stone wall several feet thick.

Metal rooflights usually arrive ready assembled, and installing them is a job any competent roofer can handle. The weakness in these units is invariably the flashing, or weather sealing, between the frame and the roof itself. It is boring but true that economies here can prove more expensive in the long run.

TOWARDS THE ATRIUM

Whereas small rooflights, like the ones we have been discussing, all related to the 'oculus', are like spotlights, underlining the internal structure and emphasizing its enclosing quality, the other sort of overhead light, the sort which harks back to the atrium, seems to open up the space beneath it, washing it with natural light, so there is a delicious sense of being at one with nature while at the same time being home and dry. As Wright's lily pad columns suggest, glazed roofs can create a mysterious sub-aqueous light, pearly, diffused and gentle, and rooms lit like this are always memorable. One of the most interesting rooms I remember was a huge sitting room made by roofing over an entire back garden, mostly with glass. There were doors, but no windows. The walls were covered with bookcases and pictures. A large fire burned in the grate. None of these things were at all out of the ordinary; what made them strange was seeing them all lit from above. The sense of seclusion, remoteness, was astonishing though the home was in the middle of the city. On fine days you could track the sun round the room, and at night you could sometimes follow the moon. It was a place with an out-of-time, magical atmosphere. Thanks, mostly, to patent glazing.

Inserting a glazed area into an existing flat-roofed space can be a solution to lightless or underlit spaces, which sometimes occur in houses or flats which have grown up piecemeal. Sometimes, too, one finds rooflights positioned above staircases. But probably the most suitable site for glazing in a large area overhead is in small city backyards, too hemmed in by buildings to enjoy much of a view or direct sunlight. Glazing over a small, dank, dark space like this, and turning it into a rooflit room, with translucent rather than clear glass, makes a plus out of a disadvantageous situation. The house acquires an extra room, and instead of a poky yard where nothing grows one has a warmed, generously lit room which can also become a successful greenhouse for plants needing an even temperature more than sunlight. Two points to watch out for if you are considering a scheme like this: the provisions for carrying off rainwater need to be carefully thought out, and the glass used needs to be the reinforced type with wire mesh sandwiched in the glass. This protects you from cats and hailstones as well as thieves. Glazing over the narrow path which runs between many back extensions and the garden wall, is another variant on this theme. The end of the 'covered way' nearest the house becomes a useful utility room/workshop while the forward end which gets the sun is a pleasant place to sit.

Design jobs involving large expanses of glass are usually best left to the professionals. Apart from the riskiness of handling large pieces of glass, which is very heavy as well as sharp, there are various problems inherent in glazed structures, like ventilation and drainage.

LANTERNS AND BELVEDERES

One particularly attractive form of rooflight, seen both from within and without a building, is the glazed lantern, quite a common feature in turn of the century houses. Lanterns are rather like a decorative little greenhouse sitting on top of your studio, hallway, garden room, or wherever, creating something of an open courtyard feeling and admitting all the available sunshine and light. Edwardian models were often tricked out with borders of coloured and 'brilliant cut' glass to increase their decorativeness. If you are fortunate enough to acquire a charming feature like this, in need of restoration, it would be worth finding a specialist firm to replace the decorative glass. Old established firms stock a huge range of coloured glass and some of them still do brilliant cutting.

Belvederes – literally, good view places – are like small glazed turrets at the top of a house where one can stand and admire an uninterrupted panoramic view. Nelson's house, on the south bank of the Thames, has a little belvedere where the admiral could keep an eye on his ships being fitted out in the nearby dock, as well as the movement of shipping up and down the river. Victor Hugo's house in Guernsey has a large, finely appointed belvedere where the exiled poet could look across the seas to France. Perched on top of a severe Georgian building, belvederes have a delightfully frivolous air. They belong to a leisured age, which is no longer with us, when gentlemen of private means could afford to indulge in expensive hobbies like astronomy.

You would have to be very wealthy today to contemplate adding a lantern, or belvedere, to an existing building. But there are patented pre-formed upstanding rooflights available which look like abstract versions of the old lantern, while others, with a hi-tech image, more resemble the nose cones of rockets. These may look less charming than their precursors, but they have all sorts of built-in technological improvements. They are often made of light-weight rust-proofed metal and clear acrylic rather than glass, which makes them lighter, tougher, and easier to install. They are designed to be opened and closed easily, and to be watertight. And, where security is a problem, they can be locked from the inside.

PUTTING IN A SKYLIGHT

If you are putting in a new skylight where there was none before you will need to go through the same procedure as when putting in new windows. It is essential, unless you are an expert builder, to have a skylight installed professionally since it is a difficult job and one which, if not done correctly, can land you with years of trouble from leaks and draughts. Make sure that you employ a reputable builder and ideally get some form of guarantee from him or withhold a portion of the money for the job until you are absolutely sure that the installation is draught and water proof.

If your skylight is being fitted into a flat roof make sure that it is installed at an angle which will allow rain to run off it rather than form pools which might eventually cause rot or damage. No flat roof is completely flat; they are always designed with a slight tilt to allow for weather and it is important that your skylight does likewise. Since hot air rises, skylights can mean that an awful lot of your expensive heat disappears out of the house fairly quickly. Install a sealed double glazed unit and, if the ceiling or roof area is fairly deep, it is worth putting another level of glass or Perspex across the opening, flush with the ceiling. Make a framework of battens around the bottom edge of the skylight opening and fit two pieces of glass or Perspex in it as this makes it easy to get the layer out when you want access to the skylight. If the area is fairly large you will find that Perspex is lighter to lift out and less likely to break than glass; an important consideration if the skylight is fairly high and you have to carry it up and down a ladder.

ACCESS

Some skylights are designed never to be opened since access through them is not required. The only problem in this instance is that you then may never be able to clean them. It is now possible to buy sliding glass roof sections which can be custom made to fit any area and which can be wound open – rather like a car sun roof – to allow air and sunshine in on fine days. A kitchen skylight of this type would be useful for dispersing smells.

Even if your skylight does not open you will need to be able to get to it regularly to clean the inside of the panes and do any necessary maintenance as well as attend to any special effects such as hanging plants. Unfortunately you cannot treat a skylight like a loft and have the kind of retractable ladder that can be hidden away inside it. So you need to buy something which is light enough to carry easily. Aluminium is the best material for this and it is best to choose the extension, self-locking type, as used by professional window cleaners, which are safe, portable and easy to store. Note that ladders should never be left outside a building where they could offer access to intruders. If you cannot store yours in a garage or shed it should be fixed to an outside wall with strong bolts that would need a lot of effort to saw through.

If your skylight is very high it is sensible to mount a fixing point for your ladder inside it so that it will stay firmly in position. This is especially important if you go through your skylight and out on to the roof; you don't want to return to find your means of descent has slipped out of its place.

CLEANING SKYLIGHTS OR ROOFLIGHTS

Cleaning any glass window is a chore, but trying to keep high, or inaccessible windows, like skylights, rooflights, lanterns, etc. sparkling is almost impossible. The modern solution, obviously worth thinking about if you are putting the windows in, rather than inheriting existing ones, is to choose a window of the swivelling type, which can be turned around completely so that the outside can be reached and cleaned from inside.

A long handled squeegee type window cleaner is your best bet, long enough to allow you to reach the window standing on a smaller step ladder, or a comforting solid piece of furniture. The gadget that swivels the window will obviously have to be extended so that it is within easy reach.

Well designed roof lanterns are often surrounded by a flat parapet on the roof, which allows them to be reached by someone with a good head for heights. Glazing of any sort set into a pitched roof is always a headache to clean, because even if

OVERLEAF: *Quirky peaked rooflights repeat the gable outlines and throw welcome light into a dark expanse in the Limehouse home built and owned by designer Thomas Brent.*

you find a clever way of crawling up a sloping roof – leaning a ladder, boards with pegs, etc. – it is liable to dislodge or damage the slates, tiles, shingles, etc. The lower levels can be reached with a long handled squeegee again, but the upper ones may have to rely on old fashioned rainwater.

SKYLIGHT SECURITY

A skylight can be a very vulnerable spot, especially if you live in a terraced house or top flat in a row of blocks, since people such as burglars can move along the roofs with no problem and break in easily. To minimise the risk of this happening ensure that your skylight is made of toughened, wired or laminated glass which will make breaking in more difficult and also decrease the risk of injury to anyone below if the glass is broken.

Make sure that the skylight is secured firmly so that it cannot be opened or raised by anyone on the roof. Bolts are a good way of doing this and also make it easy for anyone to undo from the inside, an important factor if the skylight is likely to be used as a fire escape.

DECORATIVE EFFECTS

Skylights can be treated or decorated in many imaginative ways. The glass itself may be coloured or a stained glass kit used to create a coloured design to attach to it. Shapes can be stuck to the glass to produce attractive shadows on the floor below when the sun shines.

If the skylight is in a recess rather than flush with the ceiling you could decorate the area in a number of ways, for example with one of the special paint finishes described on pages 58-62, with stencils (see page 63), with wallpaper and/or borders or some form of collage. While in some rooms it may be best to let it blend into the general decor, in others treating it as a special feature or lighting it in an interesting way may enhance the appearance of the whole room.

A skylight makes a wonderful centre for one or more hanging baskets of plants or herbs which benefit from the maximum daylight it supplies. In a kitchen you could use it as an area from which to hang baskets of fruit and vegetables or indeed pot and pans.

—SUPPLIERS—

GENERAL

Beta Naco Windows
Stourbridge Road
Bridgnorth
Shropshire
Secure louvre windows

Bolton Gate Co Ltd
Turton Street
Bolton BL1 2SP
Internal folding window grilles

British Woodworking Federation
82 New Cavendish Street
London WIM 8AD
Tel: 01-580 5588

Crittall Windows Ltd
Manor Works
Braintree
Essex CM7 6DF
Tel: 0376 24106
*Original manufacturers of steel windows in the
1920s and 1930s. Offer advice on repair and
replacement parts*

N.J.A. Gifford-Mead
The Furniture Cave
533 Kings Road
London SW10
Tel: 01-352 9904
Original stained glass windows

Hale Farm Building Materials
32 Guildford Road
Farnham
Surrey
Tel: 0252 726484
*Many types of old window including coloured and
stained glass*

Perfecta Security Shutters
5 Duxbury Hall Road
Chorley
Lancs PR7 4AT

R.W. Pike & Sons (Gloucester) Ltd
1a Daffodil Leaze
King Stanley
Glos GL10 3QL
Double glazing with fly screens

Plantation Shutters
93 Antrobus Road
Chiswick
London W4 5NQ
Tel: 01-994 2886
Range of internal pine shutters

Townsends
1 Church Street
London NW8
Tel: 01-724 3746
*Suppliers of Victorian architectural features
including stained glass windows. Also offer a
stained glass repair service.*

Vekaplast UK
Unit 7, Vale Street
Lancs BB9 OTA
Specialist windows

Weatherseal Double Glazing
Weatherseal Windows Ltd
Turner Street
Lees
Oldham
Lancs OL4 3JU
Decorated glass windows

PAINT EFFECTS

Ian Cairnie
59 Upper Tollington Park
London N4
Tel: 01-272 5367

Emma Hardie
9 Elsworthy Terrace
London NW3 3DR
Tel: 01-722 7807

Caroline Quartermaine
27c Edith Grove
London SW10
Tel: 01-351 0363

Lucinda Thomas
41 Turnstall Road
London SW9 8BZ
Gilding and paint finishes

WINDOWS

Hand Painted Stencils
6 Polstead Road
Oxford OX2 6TN
Tel: 0865 56072

Lyn le Grice Stencil Design
Bread Street
Penzance
Cornwall
Tel: 0736 69881
*Stencil catalogues on request (£1). Also
stencilling courses.*

Mary McCarthy
7 Bridge Street
Stiffkey
Wells next the Sea
Norfolk
Tel: 0328 75468

GLASS

Virginia Bliss
41 Werter Road
Putney
London SW15
Tel: 01-788 3773
Glass engraver

The British Society of Master Glass Painters
6 Queen Street
London WC1
Hon. Sec. Sheila Mole
Tel: 01-693 2417
Supplies list of members and information

Dryad Craft Centre
178 Kensington High Street
London W8
Glass engraving kits

Glass and Glazing Federation
6 Mount Row
London WIY 6DY

Goddard and Gibbs
41 Kingsland Road
London E2 8AD
Tel: 01-739 6563
*Designers, makers and installers of stained glass
windows, leaded lights etc.*

James Hetley & Co Ltd
16 Beresford Avenue
Wembley
Middx HA0 1RP
Stained glass suppliers

The Illustrated Glass Company
Unit 3, Thurston Granary
Bury St Edmunds
Suffolk IP31 3QU
Tel: 0359 32148
Sandblasted designs on glass and wooden shutters

IWF Ltd
27 Clayton Park Square
Newcastle upon Tyne
Specialist stained glass tool suppliers

Danny Lane
Glassworks
30C Camden Lock
London NW1
Tel: 01-254 9096
Sandblasting

Lead and Light
Camden Lock
Commercial Place
London NW1
Stained glass suppliers

The London Door Company
165 St Johns Hill
London SW11
Made to measure stained glass panels

Mimram Stained Glass Studio
Digswell House
Monks Rise
Welwyn Garden City
Herts
Tel: 0707 26169
Replace any kind of stained glass detailing

Maria McClafferty
119 Herne Hill
London SE24 9LY
Tel: 01-733 9146
*Designs and makes stained glass windows
and panels*

Jane McDonald
The Garden Flat
19 Osprings Road
Kentish Town
London NW5 2JD
Tel: 01-485 1240
Sandblasting and lustre processes

154

Monsanto Europe S.A.
Ave de Tervuren
270-272 B-1150 Brussels
Belgium
Laminated glass

Joseph Nuttgens
The Stained Glass Studio
Piggotts Hill
North Dean
High Wycombe
Bucks HP14 4NF
Tel: 024024 3352

Pilkington Glass Ltd
Prescot Road
St Helens
Merseyside
WA10 3TT
Numerous designs of opaque and patterned glass

James Preece
Unit 11, Portobello Green
281 Portobello Road
London W10
Tel: 01-968 8807
Modern and period stained glass windows. Also repairs old stained glass

Stained Glass Supplies Ltd
Mail order:
Unit 5, Brunel Way
Thornbury Estate
Thornbury
Avon BS12 2UR
Retail outlet:
41-49 Kingsland Road
London E2 8AD
Tel: 01-729 5661
Suppliers of all equipment and materials for stained glass and glass painting. Also instruction books and courses

Caroline Swash
88 Woodwarde Road
Dulwich
London SE22 8UT
Tel: 01-693 6574
Designs and makes stained glass windows

Worshipful Company of Glaziers
9 Montague Close
London Bridge
London SE1
Tel: 01-403 3300
Information service on all aspects of decorative glass

CURTAIN TRACKS

Antiference Ltd
Bicester Road
Aylesbury
Bucks HP19 3BJ

Curtain Plus Marketing Ltd
Earlstree Road
Corby
Northants NN17 2AZ

Graber UK Ltd
Angel Road Works
Edmonton
London N18 3AY

W.A. Hudson Ltd
115 Curtain Road
London EC2A 3QS

Hunter Douglas Ltd
15 Belsize Close
Walsall
Norton Canes
Cannock
Staffs WS11 3TQ

Silent Gliss
Star Lane
Margate
Kent CT9 4EF

Swish Products Ltd
Tamworth
Staffs B79 7TW

Winther Browne & Co Ltd
Nobel Road
Elesy's Estate
Edmonton
London N18 3DX

CURTAIN HEADINGS

Cope and Timmons Ltd
Angel Road Works
Edmonton
London N18 3AY

Rufflette Ltd
Sharston Road
Wythenshawe
Manchester

155

WINDOWS

BLIND KITS AND ACCESSORIES

Blind Alley
27 Chalk Farm Road
Camden Town
London NW1 8AG
Tel: 01-485 8030
Suppliers of all kinds of blinds. Hand paint and decorate blinds to order

Deans Blinds
Unit 4, Haslemere Industrial Estate
Ravensbury Terrace
London SW19
Tel: 01-947 8931
Ready-stiffened fabric

De Winter Ltd
223 Kensington Church Street
London W8
Tel: 01-229 1918

FABRICS AND SERVICES

CVP Designs
13 Hewer Street
London W10
Tel: 01-960 9299
Interior designers specialising in window treatment

Distinctive Trimmings
17 Kensington Church Street
London W8 4LF
Tel: 01-937 6174
Suppliers of pelmet braids and fringes, jacquard borders, tassels, tie-backs etc.

Julia Fieldwick
34 Lillieshall Road
Clapham
London SW4 0LP
Tel: 01-720 9373
Hand paints fabric and blinds

Anne Finnerty
62 Gainsborough Road
Southcote
Reading
Berks RG3 3BZ
Tel: 0734 588274
Designs and makes bead curtains, fringes etc

John Froomberg Agencies
23 Eastcastle Street
London WIN 7BP
Verosol insulating fabric

Ian Mankin
109 Regents Park Road
Primrose Hill
London NW1 8VR
Tel: 01-722 0997
Specialises in natural fabrics for furnishing

Fiona Orde Designs
19 Merthyr Terrace
London SW13 9DL
Tel: 01-748 6071
Soft furnishings designer

Paine & Co
49 Barnsbury Street
London N1 1TP
Tel: 01-607 1176
Soft furnishing designers specialising in window dressing

Putnams Antiques & Textiles
72 Mill Lane
London NW6
Tel: 01-431 2935
Furnishing fabrics based on patterns of old china

—INDEX—

157

—ACKNOWLEDGEMENTS—

Arcaid/Richard Bryant 8, 12-13, 42, 44, 150-1; Arcaid/Lucinda Lambton 39, 53, 105; Guy Bouchet Title page, 70; Michael Boys 47, 56, 57, 62, 63, 79, 96, 115, 128, 129, 133, 138, 146; Francis Carr 82; Angela Coombes 35, 37, 52, 77, 119, 124, 140, 141; CVP Designs Ltd 65, 94, 103, 113; Camera Press/Hauser 66, 80; Camera Press/Schone Wohnen 88; Esto Photographics Inc/Peter Aaron 18, 73; Susan Griggs/Michael Boys 16, 91, 100; Susan Griggs Agency/Nicholas Sapieha 4-5, 15, 25; Sonia Halliday 3; Robert Harding Picture Library/Joe Clarke 21; Robert Harding Picture Library/Christina Gascoigne 10; John Hillelson Agency/Magnum/Erich Lessing 86; Timothy Hursley/The Arkansas Office 22; Illustrated Glass Company 78; Jerrican/Daudier 123; Ken Kirkwood 32, 127; Balthazar korab 36, 43, 145; Jane McDonald 76; John Sims 14, 26, 27; Charlie Stebbings Front and back covers, 51; Studio Azzurro, Milan 28; Fritz von der Schulenberg 6, 90, 93, 98; Elizabeth Whiting Associates/Tim Street-Porter 40; The World of Interiors/Tom Leighton 89, 97, 121; The World of Interiors/Arabella McNair Wilson 142; The World of Interiors/James Mortimer 30; The World of Interiors/John Vere Brown 11; The World of Interiors/Fritz von der Schulenberg 54; The World of Interiors/James Wedge 137; ZEFA 74; ZEFA/Janoud 48